CLASSIC SERMONS
ON THE
LOVE OF GOD

KREGEL CLASSIC SERMONS Series

Classic Sermons on the Apostle Paul

Classic Sermons on the Apostle Peter

Classic Sermons on the Attributes of God

Classic Sermons on the Birth of Christ

Classic Sermons on Christian Service

Classic Sermons on the Cross of Christ

Classic Sermons on Faith and Doubt

Classic Sermons on Family and Home

Classic Sermons on Heaven and Hell

Classic Sermons on the Holy Spirit

Classic Sermons on Hope

Classic Sermons on Judas Iscariot

Classic Sermons on the Miracles of Jesus

Classic Sermons on the Names of God

Classic Sermons on Overcoming Fear

Classic Sermons on Praise

Classic Sermons on Prayer

Classic Sermons on the Prodigal Son

Classic Sermons on the Resurrection of Christ

Classic Sermons on Revival and Spiritual Renewal

Classic Sermons on the Second Coming and
    Other Prophetic Themes

Classic Sermons on the Sovereignty of God

Classic Sermons on Spiritual Warfare

Classic Sermons on Suffering

Classic Sermons on the Will of God

Classic Sermons on Worship

CLASSIC SERMONS ON THE LOVE OF GOD

Compiled by

Warren W. Wiersbe

kregel
PUBLICATIONS

Grand Rapids, MI 49501

Classic Sermons on the Love of God
Compiled by Warren W. Wiersbe

Published by Kregel Publications, a division of Kregel, Inc.,
P.O. Box 2607, Grand Rapids, MI 49501. Kregel Publications provides trusted, biblical publications for Christian
growth and service. Your comments and suggestions are
valued.

For more information about Kregel Publications, visit our
web site at http://www.kregel.com.

Cover photo: Frank Gutbrod
Cover and book design: Alan G. Hartman

Library of Congress Cataloging-in-Publication Data
Classic sermons on the love of God / Warren W. Wiersbe,
compiler.
     p.   cm.— (Kregel classic sermons series)
   Includes index.
   1. God—Love—Sermons. I. Wiersbe, Warren W.
BT140.C57   1998   231'.6—dc21   98-39122
                                         CIP
ISBN   0-8254-4083-1

CONTENTS

LIST OF SCRIPTURE TEXTS

PREFACE

THE *Kregel Classic Sermons Series* collects and publishes meaningful sermons from master preachers about significant themes.

These are *sermons,* not essays or chapters taken from books about themes. Not all of these sermons could be called great, but all of them are *meaningful.* They apply the truths of the Bible to the needs of the human heart, which is something that all effective preaching must do.

While some are better known than others, all of the preachers whose sermons I have selected had important ministries and were highly respected in their day. The fact that a sermon is included in this volume does not mean that either the compiler or the publisher agrees with or endorses everything that the man did, preached, or wrote. The sermon is here because it makes a valuable contribution.

These are sermons about *significant* themes. The pulpit is no place to play with trivia. The preacher has thirty minutes in which to help mend broken hearts, change defeated lives, and save lost souls; he can never accomplish this demanding ministry by distributing homiletical tidbits. In these difficult days we do not need clever pulpiteers who discuss the times; we need dedicated ambassadors who will preach the eternities.

The reading of these sermons can enrich your spiritual life. The studying of them can enrich your skills as an interpreter and expounder of God's truth. However God uses these sermons in your life and ministry, my prayer is that His church around the world will be encouraged and strengthened by them.

WARREN W. WIERSBE

Love's Lamentation

Charles Haddon Spurgeon (1834–1892) remains undoubtedly the most famous minister of the nineteenth century. Converted in 1850, he united with the Baptists and soon began to preach in various places. He became pastor of the Baptist church in Waterbeach, England, in 1851, and three years later he was called to the decaying Park Street Church, London. Within a short time the work began to prosper, a new church was built and dedicated in 1861, and Spurgeon became London's most popular preacher. In 1855, he began to publish his sermons weekly; today they make up the fifty-seven volumes of *The Metropolitan Tabernacle Pulpit*. He founded a pastor's college and several orphanages.

This sermon was taken from *The Metropolitan Tabernacle Pulpit,* volume 48.

Charles Haddon Spurgeon

1

LOVE'S LAMENTATION

I have loved you, saith the LORD. Yet ye say, Wherein hast thou loved us? (Malachi 1:2a).

THE CHILDREN OF ISRAEL had passed through great trouble, but all of it was brought upon them by their own sin. Yet, in their time of trouble, God had remembered them in the greatness of His grace and mercy. They had been carried into captivity in Babylon, and there they had wept when they remembered Zion. They had been scattered over the face of the earth, but God had heard their groanings. He had restored them to their own land, and given them a period of peace and prosperity. But now that they were cured of idolatry, they fell into self-righteousness, indifference, and worldlymindedness. The ordinances of God's house were neglected; or, if they were attended to outwardly, it was in such a careless, heartless manner that God was insulted by their worship rather than adored thereby.

For these reasons new sorrows were caused to fall upon them, for, under the old dispensation, it was God's rule that His obedient people were a prosperous people. But that, whenever they wandered in heart away from Him, then they began to suffer. His message to them by Moses was, "If ye will . . . walk contrary unto me, then I will walk contrary unto you also in fury; and I, even I, will chastise you seven times for your sins" (Lev. 26:27–28); so they found it. They were, therefore, now in a very sad condition, but they had no consciousness of the real cause of it. They were fretting and fuming against God instead of striking out boldly at their sins—complaining of the severity of the divine chastisement rather than confessing the iniquity by which they had brought the rod upon themselves.

So God sent His servant Malachi, the last of a long train of prophets, to seek to bring them to repentance—to try to touch their hearts and consciences by reminding them of His manifold favors, and of their base ingratitude toward Him who had treated them so graciously and with such undeserved mercy. This is to be the subject of my discourse. I want, if I can, to get at men's hearts. I shall not have much to say by way of instruction. I want rather to speak so as to impress and arouse my hearers, seeking to set your consciences at work, so that all of us—for I hope there will be something to touch us all—may be constrained to bow before God in true penitence and with genuine confession of sin.

The text seems to me to contain two things and to suggest a third. First, here is *the lamentation of love:* "I have loved you, saith the LORD." Secondly, here is *the insensibility of ingratitude:* "Yet ye say, Wherein hast thou loved us?" They would not see any signs and tokens of God's love, for they did not believe in it. And the third thing, on which I am going to speak, is *the discoveries of grace.* Though it is not in the text, the text leads us to think of it. The fifth verse tells us of it: "Your eyes shall see, and ye shall say, The LORD will be magnified from the border of Israel."

The Lamentation of Love

The lamentation is abrupt and appears to end without completing its own sense. It is the exclamation of unrequited affection: "I have loved you, saith the LORD." It is a sorrowful lament. As the eye of God rests on His rebellious people, He seems to say to them, "You are acting thus wickedly against Me, yet I have loved you. You offer polluted bread upon My altar. You bring the blind and the lame and the sick as sacrifices to Me. Thus you treat Me with derision, yet I have never treated *you* so, for 'I have loved you, saith the LORD.'" It is as if He were about to say a great deal more, but suddenly stopped. His grief would not let Him say more, so the sentence stands in its rugged majesty of pathos, "I have loved you, saith the LORD."

Taking this expression, first, in its lowest sense, namely, *the love of benevolence,* it applies to all humanity. The Lord can still say, to those who forget Him and care nothing for Him, "I have loved you." Great masses of humanity live as if there were no God. If God were really dead, it would, apparently, not make the slightest difference in their thoughts and feelings. They are, practically, dead to Him, and they act as if He were dead to them. The Lord seems to me to be speaking to some of you who never appear to have any thought about Him. He says to you, "I have treated you lovingly. I have permitted you to live and kept you in being. You are not suffering pain, the blood leaps in your veins. You are in robust and vigorous health. Yet, alas! You are spending that strength in sin. Your children have been spared to you. Your house is replete with comfort, and you have no little satisfaction in the things of this life. I gave you all these things—your corn and your wine and your oil—and I have clothed you and kept you alive. Shall I still keep on loving you in this fashion, loading you with benefits, causing you to prosper, giving you all that heart can wish? Will you, in return, continue to be hard and cold and indifferent to Me? Must I still be your Benefactor, and you remain an ingrate? Must I, from morning to night and from night to morning, visit you with kindness, and shall I never have anything from you but sullen silence and heartless indifference?"

There are some of you, who have been so prospered in the things of this world and who have been made so happy in your homes, that you ought to love the Lord who has done such great things for you. He seems to say to you, through my lips, "I have loved you. Will you never remember Me, never thank Me, never give yourself up to Me, never accept Me as your Father and your Friend?" It is a natural and just lament of love that it should have done all this, and yet should be requited by forgetfulness.

Certain men, however, go further than simply forgetting God, for they actively oppose Him. They can never seem to find language foul enough to apply to the religion of Jesus Christ. Those who are zealous on behalf of religion are described by them as cants and hypocrites, and I know not what besides. Anything like conscientiousness is ridiculed by them as pharisaism. They know better, but that is the way in which they oppose God. Yet, as He looks upon them in pity, He can say to them, "I have loved you. You oppose Me, but why do you act so?" When our Lord Jesus was upon the earth and the Jews took up stones again to stone Him, He said to them, "Many good works have I shown you from my Father; for which of those works do ye stone me?" (John 10:32). He had healed their sick, satisfied their hunger, and bestowed upon them countless boons. Yet, again and again, they took up stones to stone Him, so He said to them, "Why do you act thus toward Me?" And God might speak to many of you in similar style, and say, "I have dealt with you in love, and you have scoffed at Me, and opposed Me; but I have only met your opposition with a still greater display of love. With a strange perseverance of unappreciated and unrequited love, I have still pursued you. Then, why do you rebel against Me as you do?"

I might speak to some of you in another strain. "O, sir, your mother died rejoicing in hope. Then, why do you hate that Christ who was her joy and delight? Has the Lord Jesus Christ ever made your children become unkind to you? Has He ever been the means of any wrong being done to you?" You know that it has not been so, but that all His influence among the sons of men has been for the good of the whole commonwealth, and for the establishment of peace and righteousness the wide world over. Why, then, do men oppose Him so fiercely? Some of them seem almost to foam at the mouth whenever they mention His sacred name. Well may He, then, as He looks upon the atheist and the Socinian, say to them, as He says to so many more, "I have treated you with love, yet this is the only return I receive from you. Shall it always be so?"

The same expression may be used concerning the many who have long heard the Gospel, and who yet remain unsaved. Now I can speak personally to a great many of you who are here. God has indeed shown His love to you in permitting you to meet with us in this house of prayer. You might have been born in some far-off country where you would have been taught the abominations of paganism, or Romanism, or Mohammedanism. The name of Jesus might never have been sounded in your ears. Yet it has been, and with many of you from your very childhood. I will not speak in praise of my own ministry, but I will say this—I have always preached the Gospel to the best of my ability. All that I have known of the Word of God, I have spoken. I have tried to use the best words that I could get together in proclaiming the Gospel message. And seeing that so many hundreds, and even thousands, have found the Lord Jesus Christ here, I am right in saying that you have been in a highly privileged place. You have had opportunities given to you that are denied to a great many people, and God has proved that He has loved you in giving you such privileges. If you still remain hearers only and not doers of the Word, I can fancy my Lord and Master weeping over you as He wept over Jerusalem when He said, "How often would I have gathered thy children together, even as a hen gathereth her chickens under her wings, and ye would not!" (Matt. 23:37b).

The words of our text will also be applicable to many when they come to die. When God comes to look back upon the whole of a man's life, and to recall the way in which he has treated that man from the first day of his history to the last, He will be able to say to many a man who will die unregenerate, "Yet, I loved you. I put you into the arms of a woman who taught you to fear My name. I placed you in circumstances that ought to have led you to thought, to prayer, to repentance, and to faith. I have preserved your life and cared for you, until now that you lie there dying, and you will be lost because of despised mercy and unrequited love. I called, but you refused. I stretched out My hand, but you regarded not. Now you are lost and must be driven away from My presence forever, not because I treated you roughly, or denied to you the message of salvation, or shut you out of heaven, but because you yourselves spurned My love, and set at naught all My entreaties."

I think I told you, once, the story of a godly woman who was wonderfully kind to her very unkind and wicked husband. She was so obedient, gentle, affectionate, and patient that he even boasted about what a good wife he had. In company one night, long past the hour of midnight, he said that if he took his drunken companions home with him, late as it was, she would receive them like a lady. He boasted that she would prepare a supper for them and never show by word or sign that it was hard upon her, or that they were not welcome. And it came true. When he took them home, she got together such things as she had and made a decent feast for them. One of them addressed her afterward and said that they had come there as the result of a wager. He stated that they could not understand how she could have patience with such a man as her husband was, for they themselves felt ashamed of the way he had acted toward her. When they pressed her for her answer, she said with tears, "I am afraid that my husband's only happiness will be in this life. I have prayed for him and sought in vain to bring him to a better mind. My fear is that, when this life is over, there will be no more happiness for him, so I mean to make him as happy as ever he can be in his present condition."

It seems to me that God sometimes acts upon that plan, for He gives to some men more than heart can wish. Their eyes stand out with fatness, and He multiplies to them all earthly blessings. Because He is a God who would make men as happy as they can be, He will let them have happiness here, for, in the eternity to come, it will not be possible for His justice to deal out anything to them but those sorrows that are the inevitable consequence of perseverance in sin.

Even in this first part of my theme, there seems to me to be much that ought to touch many hearts. But when I come to *the higher sense of the term "love"* and speak of God's own chosen people, to whom He can with emphasis say, "I have loved you," oh, how sad it is that the Lord has often to say this to them while they are in their unregenerate state! He has chosen them to eternal life. He has written their names in the Lamb's book of life. His well-beloved Son has already bought them with His precious blood. Yet look at them—slaves to lust, rioting in sin, or merely hearers of the Word, but not doers of it, still rejecting the Savior and continually going from bad to worse. Oh, could someone only echo in their ears this little message of God, "I have loved you." Could they—would they—remain as they are, without the love of God shed abroad in their hearts or any desire to be drawn toward Him? God knows all about His eternal love toward them, and the choice that He has made of them. Often must He say, as He beholds their heart of stone and brow of brass and neck of steel, "Yes, I have loved you, O you poor foolish creatures. You shall yet be mine and shall sing among the angels, though now you are rioting in sin and reveling in iniquity!" I think I hear the Lord thus graciously expressing the inmost feelings of His heart, and the very repetition of the message ought to touch all our hearts

But, further, think how the Lord must express Himself, in a similar style, concerning wandering backsliders. There are some whom we have every reason to regard as His people. In times past they have given abundant evidence that they were His, but they have grown spiritually cold, as if a death-chill had struck them in their heart. They have, apparently, gone back to the world, and they are now far off from the place where they used to be. But the Lord looks upon them in their wretchedness and sin, and He says to them, "I have loved you. You may be trying to live without prayer, but I have loved you. You may have ceased to frequent the house of God, but I have loved you. 'I remember thee, the kindness of thy youth, the love of thine espousals, when thou wentest after me in the wilderness, in a land that was not sown' (Jer. 2:2). 'Can a woman forget her sucking child, that she should not have compassion on the son of her womb? Yea, they may forget, yet will I not forget thee' (Isa. 49:15). 'Turn, O backsliding children, saith the LORD; for I am married unto you' (Jer. 3:14a)."

"The LORD, the God of Israel, saith that he hateth

putting away" (Mal. 2:16a). He has not sued for a divorce from His unfaithful spouse, as He might well have done. "Only acknowledge thine iniquity" (Jer. 3:13a), says He, confess "that thou hast transgressed against the LORD, thy God," and thou shalt be fully and freely forgiven, for He has loved thee.

I pray that my blessed Master may Himself speak to any poor backslider who is here, for, surely, His gentle, gracious accents ought to melt even a heart of stone. If you ever were really His, however far you may have wandered from Him, do not hesitate to come back to Him, for He still says to you, "I have loved you." Yes, dear friends, whenever any of the Lord's people get into a sad, lean, low condition—when they begin to grow cold and to doubt whether they can be the children of God at all—it is well for them to hear the great Father say to them, again and again, "I have loved you; I have loved you; I have loved you. I, who made the heavens and the earth, have loved you. I have loved you from before the foundation of the world. I have not merely pitied you, as a man might pity a starving dog, but I have loved you with all My heart. I have loved many others besides you. But, still, I have as much love for you as if there were nobody else for Me to love in all the world." Surely, God will cause this simple but most comforting truth to come home to the hearts of His people. Then they will cry, "We will arise and go to our Father, and confess our wanderings and our sins, that we may once more be at peace with Him."

Are you, dear friend, very sorrowful just now? Have you lost the light of God's countenance? Are you sighing and crying for the peace you once enjoyed? Well, then, just do what I have been bidding the sinner do. Come to Christ over again and, at the same time, make diligent inquiry to find out whether there is any wrong thing in your character that is bringing you into this state of misery. How long is it since you have thoroughly swept out the secret chambers of your heart? If you leave a room unswept for a little while, you know how the cobwebs and the dust gather and settle all over it. Look even at the snow after it has been lying for a day or two in such a foggy, smoky, grimy city as London; it is positively black. Well, if the snow gets black in this smoke, do you not think that your soul will also get foul and dirty? This world is a bad place to live in. To maintain a high condition of purity you will need a deal of grace, or you certainly will not do it. Ah, me! How little there is around us that can help us toward God, and how much there is to draw us away from Him! Now, because of all this impurity by which you are surrounded, your soul needs to be constantly swept out. You had better cry to the Holy Spirit to light the candle and frequently sweep out the room, for, unless there is a constant cleansing, there will be continual filth. Then the heart will never be fit for Christ to come into it and to abide in it.

So much, then, concerning the lamentation of love.

The Insensibility of Ingratitude

There is a very cruel response to God's assurance of His love in our text; can you detect the heartless ingratitude in it? I am afraid I do not know how to pronounce the words aright so as to bring out all the evil that is in them. First, you hear God saying, in very plaintive tones, "I have loved you." Then, instead of that declaration touching the hearts of those who had wandered from Him, and constraining them to ask for mercy at His hands, you get this wicked question, "Wherein hast thou loved us?" That is all the reply they give. It is short and sharp, full of unbelief and pride and rebellion: "Wherein hast thou loved us?" Does anybody ever ask that question of God nowadays? Oh, yes! I have heard it many times.

That question is sometimes asked by *men who are loaded with temporal mercies*. There is nothing that God has denied to them. When they were younger, if anybody had told them that they would be worth as much as they now actually possess, they would have said that it was beyond their utmost expectations. Yet now that they have all that their heart can desire, and their eyes stand out with fatness, they put to God this shameful question,

"Wherein hast thou loved us?" They say that they cannot see any sign of the goodness of God in their prosperity; they trace all their riches and their increase to their own wit, wisdom, industry, and perseverance, but they leave God out of the matter altogether. And so, although His mercies stare them in the face, and they wear the tokens of those mercies on their backs and carry them within their physical frame, yet they continue to say to Him, "Wherein hast thou loved us?"

I have known others who have practically said the same thing by *the way in which they have slighted gospel privileges*. A man of this stamp, who has been a hearer of the Gospel for, perhaps, twenty or thirty years, says, "I do not see any proofs of any particular favor that God has shown to me." O sir, if you had been cast into hell, you would have learned to prize the privilege of listening to the Gospel when you had lost it forever! If you had been, for even a little while, in a lunatic asylum, when you came out you might begin rightly to value the blessing of restored reason, with which you are able to understand at least something of that Gospel that you have so long neglected and despised. It is strange that there should be people living on praying ground and on pleading terms with God, with heaven to be had for the asking, who yet say to the Lord, "Wherein hast thou loved us?" Ah, some of you see what kings and prophets desired to see, but died without the sight. Yet you say to God, "Wherein hast thou loved us?" How happy ought to be your ears that hear the Gospel's joyful sound, yet, as you hear it not in your hearts, you cry to the Lord, "Wherein hast thou loved us?"

Yes, and I have heard this question put very bitterly by *some who have murmured at their temporal trials*. "How has God been gracious to us?" they say. "Look at me," says one, "I am very poor. I work as hard as any slave, yet I get but little return for all my toil. My lot is a truly pitiable one. In what respects has God loved me?" "Look," says another, "at this broken leg." Or perhaps the lament is, "I was born deformed"; or, "I lost an eye early in life. Don't talk to me about God loving me." Yet there are many, now in heaven, who might never have gone there if it had not been for their poverty, their infirmity, and their pain. Often, when God is hedging up a man's way with thorns to stop him from going to destruction, he thinks that the Lord is unkind to him, whereas the thorns in the way are the surest tokens of divine love to him. Yes, you were once able to drink greedily from the muddy stream of worldly pleasure, and you kept on at it as long as you could. I do not know where you might have been by this time had not God struck you down, taken away your power of enjoyment, and deprived you of the means by which you indulged yourself in sin. What better service could He have rendered to you? The silly, self-willed child will not thank his father for the rod. But when he becomes a man, if that rod has been really useful to him, he will respect and love the wise and kind father who did not spare him for all his crying. And you, dear friend, who are in trouble and sorrow, say that God is dealing harshly with you, yet those trials are all sent in love. That sharp affliction of yours is the surgeon's knife that is cutting away the proud flesh and deadly cancers which, otherwise, would destroy you. God is working for your good in all that He is doing; it is His love that is doing it all.

I am sorry to say that I have known some, who appeared to be the Lord's people, who have said to Him, "Wherein hast thou loved us?" because they have become very doubting. They have not looked at eternal things, they have kept looking at their outward inconveniences and sorrows. The poor man has said, "With this leaky roof to my cottage, can God really love me?" And the poor woman has said, "With this rheumatism in my aching bones, and poor little children half clad and ill fed, can God really love me?" And even the heirs of heaven have sometimes asked of God, "Wherein hast thou loved us?" But when they have come back to their right mind and have rightly understood the ways of the Lord, they have blessed Him for their troubles as much as for their joys. They have seen how all things work together for good to them that love God.

It shows how wrong is the state of our heart if we can live in the midst of God's continued mercies, and yet cannot realize that He loves us. If any of you cannot see any tokens of the benevolence and goodness of God to you, surely you must be blind. If, dear child of God, you fail to perceive what the Lord has done for you, anoint your eyes with salve that you may see, for He has done everything for you. He has given you this world, and worlds to come. Aye, and He has given Himself to you to be your Father, His Son to be your Savior, and His Spirit to be your constant Comforter. What more can He do for you than He has done, you who have fled for refuge to lay hold of the hope set before you in the Gospel? Therefore, never let this thought flit across your soul, and never let this question pass the door of your lips, "Wherein hast thou loved us?"

Thus have I spoken upon the insensibility of ingratitude as well as the lamentation of love.

The Discoveries of Grace

I am hoping and praying that these last words I am about to utter may come true in the experience of a great many in this place, as well as of others who will read the discourse when it is printed.

Suppose you should be converted—become a child of God and be saved. The first thing you will discover will be that *God has loved you*. What a change that will make in all your feelings toward Him! You will never again say to the Lord, "Wherein hast thou loved me?" But, if you feel as I did when I first found out the love of God to me, you will begin tracing your whole history, from your cradle up to the moment of your conversion, and you will say, "I can see the Lord's loving hand there, and there, and there, and there, and there." You will look upon your trials, your losses, your crosses, your removals from one village or town to another, and you will say, "Ah! it was love that watched over me all the while. It was love that was arranging all that happened for my good." And you will be amazed at the difference that feeling will make in your life. Before you knew the Lord, you could not realize His love. But, as soon as ever you really know Him, you will say, "All His dealings with me have been proofs of His love." You will put up your hands in wonder and say, "How could I have been such a mad fool as to go on sinning against God in spite of such wondrous love? It really seems to me now as if, the more I sinned, the more He loved me. The worse I was to Him, the better He was to me. Over against my black sin, He set the whiteness and brightness of His grace. He seemed as if He conquered me, not by the sheer force of His might, but by the superior power of His boundless love."

Further, if you shall be converted, it will not be long before you will find out that, in addition to God being loving and kind to you in His providence, *He so loved you that He gave His only-begotten Son to die for you.* The general truth that Christ died for sinners is unspeakably precious, but the sweetest truth in all the world is for any one of us to be able to say, "He died for me." O my dear hearer, if you were ever to find out that Christ thought of you in His last moments upon the cross—that He distinctly and personally poured out His life for you and that your name—I mean, your very own name—is graven upon the palms of His hands, and that You, in your own person, are continually before Him—surely that would be a heartbreak for you. All the law and the terrors in the world might only harden you in your rebellion, but one glance of the dear languid eyes of Him who hung upon the cross—one gracious look of His—will make your spirit flow like the streams of water that ran out of the rock in the wilderness. May the Lord, in His mercy, enable each one of you to say, "[He] loved me and gave himself for me" (Gal. 2:20b), for then you will soon be at His feet as weeping, yet rejoicing, penitents.

Again, if you are really converted, so that you come to know the love of God and the redemption that is in Christ Jesus, another thing that you will soon find out will be *God's election of you from eternity.* How well I recollect when first that ray of light struck into my soul, as I seemed to hear Him say to me personally, "I have loved thee with an everlasting love; therefore, with loving-kindness have I drawn thee" (Jer. 31:3). That great truth was revealed to me in this way. I said to myself, "Here am I converted, pardoned, saved. There are my school fellows, the boys and young men with whom I used to be associated, and they are not saved. Who has made the difference between us?" I dared not say that I had, and so put the crown of salvation on my own head. I saw, in a single moment, that God must have made the distinction if I was, in any degree whatsoever, different from my fellow-creatures. Then I said to myself, "If God has made this difference in me and done more for me than He has done for others, there must always have been in His heart thoughts of love toward my soul, since He never changes. What He does today, is the result of the purpose that was in His heart from before the foundation of the world." So there rolled into my heart, like a stream of honey, the assurance that He had loved me, with complacency, long before the earth was formed, or the day-star knew its place, or planets ran their round.

Then I said to myself, "O you fool of fools, that you should ever have treated your God as you have done! Are you indeed one of His elect and chosen people, and yet have you lived all these years without hardly a thought of Him who has loved you from eternity?" I blamed myself, as I do still, that I was so slow to recognize His eternal choice of me. If the Lord shall be pleased to say to you in the words of my text, "I have loved you"—when you once really know His love to you, His redemption of you, and His election of you personally—you will no more say, "Wherein hast thou loved me?" But you will bow, in speechless but grateful reverence, at His dear feet, worshiping and adoring the greatness of His infinite love.

I do not know how you feel, brothers and sisters who know the Lord, but I feel that if I could live a thousand lives, I would like to live them all for Christ. I would even then feel that they were all too little a return for His great love to me. And if any of us could have grace and strength enough given to us to die a thousand deaths for Christ, He well deserves them for having loved us as He has done.

There are just two things that I want to say to you, and with them I will finish my discourse.

First, some of you are still living in sin. Perhaps you hardly know why you came to the Tabernacle tonight. Possibly, it was only out of curiosity. I am no thought reader, but I can imagine that some of you have been in the habit of pooh-poohing all religion, ridiculing it. You have done so for a long while. Now, suppose that one of these days you should preach the very faith that you now despise, just as the apostle Paul did. Do not utter more words than you can help in reply to this suggestion of mine, for you will have to eat them up, however many there are of them. Do not go any further in the wrong road than you can help, because you will have to come all that way back. I dare to tell you, in my Master's name, that some of you who hate Him will love Him before long. Though now you oppose Him all you can, by-and-by you will be among the first to vindicate His cause. My Lord knows all about you. As He has bought you with His precious blood, do you think He will not claim you as His own? He has written your name in His book of life, so the Devil himself and all his legions cannot take from you the life everlasting to which His predestinating grace has ordained you. You shall yet bow down before Him.

The day draws near when you, who talk in a hectoring fashion now, will be found lying at His feet as suppliants. Then, when He has drawn you to Himself and has favored you with much of His love, when one of these Sunday nights you shall be found sitting at His table and the spikenard shall give forth a sweet smell, and your very soul shall seem to be carried away to heaven because of the presence of your Beloved, I wonder what you will think of yourself then? Suppose He were then to whisper in your ear (I know He will not do so.), and He were to remind you of all your ill behavior toward Him—He will not do so because He gives "liberally, and upbraideth not" (James 1:5). But suppose your own memory should be your accuser and should say to you, "Remember that you were a bondslave in the land of Egypt. Recollect those black sins that came out of your heart, those foul words that issued from your lips." Do you not think that as you look up into the face of Jesus, your Lord and Master, you will say, "Ah, my gracious Savior, I have thought of a fresh reason for loving You. I knew it before, but it has come home to me more vividly now than ever: Should not they love most who have had most forgiven? That is my case, my Lord; therefore, bind me to Yourself, and let me never again wander away from You, but let me love You even to the end."

And lastly, dear friends, I wonder what we shall think of ourselves when we get away from communion with the saints on earth and sit up yonder with our Savior in heaven. There is one who was once a drunkard. What a strange thing it will be for him to find himself in heaven! Here he was stuttering and stammering, and could not speak plainly because of his drunkenness, but he has been washed and cleansed in the blood of Jesus, and there he is singing more sweetly even than the angels. Would you believe it? That very man up there—that bright spirit, robed in white, who sings the loudest of them all, used to curse and swear, and ill-treat his wife because she went to the house of God. Yet there he is, purified and glorified. See what sovereign grace can do! But what must he think of himself when he gets up there?

I was trying to imagine what must be the emotion of such a man as Paul, who had been a persecutor and injurious, when he looks into the face of his dear Lord and Master, and casts his crown before Him, and yet all the while thinks, "But I persecuted Him!" I wonder whether that man is there who pierced His side and those soldiers who nailed Him to the tree. Certainly, he is there who railed at Him on the cross, then repented, and was forgiven. He is there who said, "I know not the man" (Matt. 26:74). When they are singing, "Worthy is the Lamb that was slain to receive power, and riches, and wisdom, and strength, and honor, and glory, and blessing" (Rev. 5:12), I think that, sometimes, Peter pauses a while and those around wonder why Peter has left off singing, but he cannot help it. Emotions of unutterable gratitude are coming over him as he remembers that he has been forgiven through the wondrous grace of Christ, who loved him even when He was being denied by him with oaths and curses.

I wish that I could communicate to you the emotions of my own spirit as I think of the greatness of humanity's sin and set it side by side with the greatness of God's grace—as I think of love unspeakable and of sin unutterably vile, which that love puts away. Come, dear friends, and let us all join together to bless and magnify the wondrous love that God has revealed to us in His Word. May we all meet in heaven, to the praise of the glory of His grace, for His dear Son's sake! Amen.

Love's Supreme Disclosure

William M. Clow (1853–1930) was born in Scotland and educated in Auckland, New Zealand, and Glasgow. From 1881 to 1911 he pastored five churches in Scotland and then joined the faculty of the United Free Church College in Glasgow. He taught theology for several years and closed his ministry as principal of the college. *The Cross in Christian Experience* and *The Day of the Cross* are two of his most popular books.

This sermon was taken from *The Cross in Christian Experience,* published in 1908 by Eaton and Mains, New York.

William M. Clow

2

LOVE'S SUPREME DISCLOSURE

God is love. In this was manifested the love of God toward us, because that God sent his only begotten Son into the world, that we might live through him (1 John 4:8b–9).

LOVE IS IMPOSSIBLE of definition. Yet you all know what love is. As children your hearts went out unquestioningly to those whose faces bent over you in tenderness. As young men and women your spirits awoke to that enthralling passion of delight and desire whose memory will be fragrant to your oldest years. As you have grown older, you have been bound by strong cords of yearning affection to your children, until your hearts tremble when a shadow falls across their lives. There is a love that is purer still, that unspeakably solemn love for the dead. When we are asked, "What is this pure passion of delight, of imperial control, with its strange power to purify and exalt?" we answer, "Love is that insight and sympathy that craves to bless and delights to commune." It is that sense of need that can be satisfied only by giving. It is a quenchless desire for the well-being of the beloved. In a perfection of which we cannot even dream, God is Love. Because God is this insight and sympathy and delight and desire, He has made a supreme disclosure of Himself. "In this was manifested the love of God toward us, because that God sent his only begotten Son into the world, that we might live through him."

Now love, as John tells us again and again, is to be seen and known only in what it does. We shall therefore look at this love of God, disclosing itself in lovely deeds, and rise step by step to see the supreme disclosure in the Cross of Christ.

Love Is a Social Passion

There cannot be love without at least two, a lover and a beloved. The man who had never seen the face of a fellowman could not know the meaning of love. The faculty of love would be dormant in him and be felt only as an unsatisfied yearning. If God be love, He must have loved from all eternity. Before the angels were created or the universe had being, God was love. God never dwelt in a still and awful loneliness. Heaven was never a cloister of hermit silence. Heaven was always a home of fellowship and a sanctuary of praise. People find the great truth of the Trinity difficult to comprehend, and more difficult to state. But it lies clear, entrancing, comforting in the light of the message that God is love.

There was love between the Father and the Son, and between the Father and the Spirit before time began to be. When the Son emptied Himself of His glory, the most costly sacrifice was not that He took our flesh and was found in fashion as a man. This was the supreme loss, and the heaviest sorrow, that, as one passes out of the love and communion of a home into a hard and alien world, so Christ passed out from the Father into the scorn of Nazareth and the outcastness of Nazareth and Jerusalem. This truth throbs through His high-priestly prayer with an accent of pain. The intense moment of that prayer is not reached when Jesus speaks of "the glory which I had with thee before the world was" (John 17:5). It is reached in that climax of His longing when He recalls the love wherewith "thou lovedst me before the foundation of the world" (v. 24). Before time began God is love, for love is a social passion.

Love Is Creation

Love must create, and it must create well-being. Love cannot be inactive. It must plan and toil and spend its resources and exert its energy. It must devise order, goodness, beauty, joy. Here we have the mighty motive of creation. Love is the source, and creation is the stream. God does not love the world simply because He created it. He created this world of life and beauty and order because He is love. It is always love that builds a home. It is always love that makes a garden. It is always love that peoples a wilderness.

The first words of the Bible are a revelation of love: "In the beginning God created the heaven and the earth" (Gen. 1:1). Lift your eyes and see the beauty of the world; walk abroad on a summer's dewy dawn; mark the evening light fading into infinite azure; look up at the hills or stand by the seashore; gladden your eyes by the sight of the valleys covered over with corn. You all find strength and solace in such communion with nature. But do you remember not only that God is the maker and builder of it all, but that it was love that caused Him to make and to build?

This more—you shall remember that God is a personal love. He cannot be satisfied with a fair and ordered universe of things.

> So sing old worlds, and so
> New worlds that from Thy footstool go.

Browning finely conceives God to say the above when He craves His little human praise. For love seeks response, and so God said, "Let us make man in our image, after our likeness" (Gen. 1:26). When next you ponder the things of your spirit, your faculties of love and joy and hope; when you fear and sorrow and pray; when you hunger and thirst for more than this world can give, you shall realize with a strengthening joy that God created you with your spiritual capacity to respond to Him because He is love.

Love Is Providence

Love cannot be content with creation. It must pass on to care, and God's care is His providence. Your little son makes himself a rudely shaped boat. Its designing has filled his heart and busied his hand for hours. At length he launches his little mimic craft by some beach. Does he set his venture afloat and then turn his back upon it, heedless of its fate? Mark how he waits and watches and risks himself lest his little vessel come to untimely shipwreck. Love created it, and love hangs over it in absorbing care.

And so God did not create the universe, make all things beautiful in their season, and set His Spirit in man, and then turn His back and vanish into silence. He does not sit afar off on the world's edge to see it go. The world is not a piece of clockwork, finished once for all and set agoing by an almighty mechanic. It is a living and growing organism. God's eyes are ever watching it. His fingers are ever working upon it. His hands ever devising new beauty in it. What sunshine there is in a thought like that! It is not difficult to believe in God the Creator. It is almost impossible not to believe. The materialist may think his way back through a few stages of the world's progress, but he comes at length to the wall that blocks his way. The only open door in that wall is the great word—God.

But it is more difficult to believe in God as providence. There is so much that is amiss in the world and in human life. Nature is red in tooth and claw. Storms desolate the earth. Pestilence and famine fill the graves with untimely dead. Youth is blighted in its bloom. Old age is often a weariness and a sorrow. Even the moral order of the world seems so imperfect. There are wars in which brutal might prevails. There are tyrannies that endure. There are nameless sorrows that quench the joy of simple and trustful hearts. But when you stand upon this mountain peak and remember that God is love, and that love's highest purpose is the well-being of the beloved, all that looks so dark lies in clear light.

What is nature, with its mingled sunshine and shadow, blight and bloom, but God's school? What is circumstance but His lesson book? What is the world with its constant call for service but His workshop? The struggle and strain and peril and vicissitude of the world are only God's tools. As the simplest and yet wisest of all Christian poets wrote in his direst extremity—

> Behind a frowning providence
> He hides a smiling face.

Love Is Grace

This is where love makes its supreme disclosure. What is grace but love dealing with sin? How does love always deal with sin? What have fathers and mothers done for their wasteful and prodigal children? What have husbands and wives done for those who have filled their secret hours with sorrow, and thwarted them in every pure and holy purpose? What have friends done, in long-continuing patience and in impoverishing service, for those who have broken promise after promise, frustrated every self-denying effort, and plunged willfully into iniquity? What can love do for sin but spend itself in redemption? The unwritten histories and the untold secrets of every family are the stories of the costly effort at redeeming its prodigals. The unknown sacrifices of many a reticent man and silent woman are those that are made, day after day, to win dear ones back to purity and truth. What can God, who is love, do for the sinner but pour Himself out in costly sacrifice to redeem him?

What a flood of light this casts on the Gospel and the cross of Christ! All men wonder at the widening dominion and deepening significance of the person of Christ. It is the strangest marvel of all time that the obscure Carpenter of Nazareth, and the peasant Prophet of Galilee, and the Crucified of Jerusalem is not the only outstanding figure of the past, but the mightiest force and personality of the present. Yet how beset with difficulty the story is! Have you never stumbled at the Virgin birth and found the Incarnation—God manifest in the flesh—a trial to your faith? Have you not found the record of those stainless years under the Syrian blue, which came to their consummation in an uncomforted sorrow and a deserted shame, a greater mystery than any other event of time? Can you stand below the cross and always find its atonement an easy message to receive?

But when you read the great words, "In this was manifested the love of God toward us, because that God sent his only begotten Son into the world, that we might live through him." "Herein is love, not that we loved God, but that he loved us, and sent his Son to be the propitiation for our sins" (1 John 4:10), all lies in light. The birth and the life and the death of Christ are seen to be God's supreme disclosure of His love. You realize what it means for a spirit of infinite holiness to be also a spirit of infinite love. The manger and the cross are only love stooping to redeem.

Love Is Discipline

Love's supreme disclosure is the cross, but love which redeems must pass on to discipline. Love's redeeming work was not done when Christ had burst the gates of hell. The dominion of sin was broken, but its fascination and power were not wholly annulled. No man who has accepted the forgiveness of God, and put himself under the mastership of Christ, can be ignorant that the power of indwelling sin is his most humbling experience. There is a work of God for man. There is also a work of God in man. Therefore God disciplines His redeemed. He chastens by mercy and by judgment, through limiting privation and burdening care, by the shadow on the heart and the thorn in the flesh, to purify and to perfect in righteousness.

The problems of life find a solution, and its dark experiences gleam with beauty when we see them in this light. Asaph found that his feet were almost gone and his steps had nearly slipped when he saw the prosperity of the wicked (Psalm 73). The author of the Book of Job left its problem of undeserved affliction unsolved. It was a mystery too dark for one who had not seen Christ's day. It is his glory that he made a meek submission when he could not even dimly understand. We are all at times sick at heart over the dark calamities and the strange anomalies of life. Men's faith falters over their long continuing sorrows, their unsatisfied hungers, their unredressed wrongs. How can God be love when He compels us to walk in such darkness and heat? How can God be love when He permits such sufferings to fall upon the innocent? How can God be love when so many lives are lived in hopeless anguish?

We forget, for one thing, that there are other wills and other powers in the world besides the will and the power of God. But we forget this, most of all, that because God is love, He is discipline. His purpose is not the pleasing of our flesh; His design is not that we should live in soft luxury. "For this is the will of God, even your sanctification" (1 Thess. 4:3a)—the final redemption of body, soul, and spirit. It is the indwelling within you of that hope and joy in God which are eternal life. This is love's final aim in the sending of the Son, "That we might live through him" (1 John 4:9). Therefore God as a husbandman uses His pruning knife. Therefore, He sits as a refiner watching His purifying fires. Therefore He chastens and scourges and corrects as a father chastens his son. His will is to make us to be partakers of His holiness and to be conformed to the image of His Son.

Love Is Heaven

In the New Testament teaching, that is the issue of love's work in the Cross and by the discipline of God. Love can never be satisfied without the loved one's presence and fellowship. "I go to prepare a place for you. . . . that where I am, there ye may be also" (John 14:2–3), was the last assurance of incarnate love. To that message all the New Testament writers make a yearning response. "Now we see through a glass, darkly; but then face to face" (1 Cor. 13:12), wrote the apostle whose quenchless hope was to see the face of Christ. "God is not ashamed to be called their God, for he hath prepared for them a city" (Heb. 11:16) is the cry of another, who saw in his vision the cloud of witnesses in the presence of God. "We shall see him as he is" (1 John 3:2), declared a third, who looked forward to sitting down again to meet with his Lord. Immortality may have many reasons to support it, but it rests ultimately on that love which has called us friends and will not let us go. It depends on that love which will suffer separation and absence only for "a little while" (John 16:16–19).

I find that the faith and hope of heaven have declined of late. I find that even the explicit testimony of Christ

is ceasing to have weight with some. The thought of
heaven has become too great, and the thought of hell too
dark for fearful hearts. But because I am assured that
God is love, and craves the presence and communion of
His beloved, and because I know Him to be righteousness who cannot tolerate sin, I am convinced both of
heaven and hell. Jesus will not let Peter and John and
Paul, and Mary of Nazareth and Mary of Bethany and
Mary Magdalene pass into dust and oblivion. Their spirits have gone to God who loved them. There cannot be
only one state and one place for Mary and for Judas, for
the penitent and for the impenitent thief, for the saintly
men and women you and I have known, and for the willful and cynical lovers of lust and crime. I am persuaded
that every man in this world is on pilgrimage, either to
the presence and communion of God, or to those presences of discord and hate in the outer darkness without
the gate.

Have you known and believed the love that God has
toward us? Do you sometimes long for that simple and
unquestioning faith in God's love which you had when
you knelt at your mother's knee? That you cannot have.
God has a better thing in store for you. In the things of
love as much as in the things of faith and hope you must
put away childish things. God has this message for you,
which meets all the breadth of your adulthood's thoughts
and all the depth of your adulthood's needs: He is love
eternal, love that creates, love that provides, love that
redeems, love that disciplines, love that waits to bid us
welcome to the Father's home at last—

> God loves to be longed for, He longs to be sought,
> For He sought us Himself with such longing and love,
> He died for desire of us, marvellous thought!
> And He yearns for us now to be with Him above.

NOTES

Immeasurable Love

Charles Haddon Spurgeon (1834–1892) remains
undoubtedly the most famous minister of the nineteenth
century. Converted in 1850, he united with the Baptists
and soon began to preach in various places. He became
pastor of the Baptist church in Waterbeach, England, in
1851, and three years later he was called to the decaying
Park Street Church, London. Within a short time the
work began to prosper, a new church was built and
dedicated in 1861, and Spurgeon became London's most
popular preacher. In 1855, he began to publish his
sermons weekly; today they make up the fifty-seven
volumes of *The Metropolitan Tabernacle Pulpit*. He
founded a pastor's college and several orphanages.

This sermon was taken from *The Metropolitan
Tabernacle Pulpit,* volume 31.

Charles Haddon Spurgeon

3

IMMEASURABLE LOVE

For God so loved the world, that he gave his only begotten Son, that whosoever believeth in him should not perish, but have everlasting life (John 3:16).

I WAS VERY GREATLY SURPRISED the other day, in looking over the list of texts from which I have preached, to find that I have no record of ever having spoken from this verse. This is all the more singular because I truly say that it might be put in the forefront of all my volumes of discourses as the sole topic of my life's ministry. It has been my one and only business to set forth the love of God to men in Christ Jesus. I heard lately of an aged minister of whom it was said, "Whatever his text, he never failed to set forth God as love, and Christ as the atonement for sin." I wish that much the same may be said of me. My heart's desire has been to sound forth, as with a trumpet, the good news that "God so loved the world, that he gave his only begotten Son, that whosoever believeth in him should not perish, but have everlasting life."

We are about to meet around the communion table, and I cannot preach from this text anything but a simple gospel sermon. Can you desire a better preparation for communion? We have fellowship with God and with one another upon the basis of the infinite love that is displayed in Jesus Christ our Lord. The Gospel is the fair white linen cloth that covers the table on which the communion feast is set. The higher truths—those truths that belong to a more enlightened experience, those richer truths that tell of the fellowship of the higher life— all these are helpful to holy fellowship, but I am sure not more so than those elementary and foundation truths which were the means of our first entrance into the kingdom of God. Babes in Christ and men in Christ here feed upon one common food. Come, aged saints, be children again. You that have long known your Lord, take up your first spelling book and go over your A-B-C's again by learning that God so loved the world that He gave His Son to die that man might live through Him.

I do not call you to an elementary lesson because you have forgotten your letters, but because it is a good thing to refresh the memory, and a blessed thing to feel young again. What the old folks used to call the Christ-cross Row contained nothing but the letters of the alphabet, yet all the books in the language are made out of those letters. Therefore, do I call you back to the cross and to Him who bled thereon. It is a good thing for us all to return at times to our starting place and make sure that we are in the way everlasting. The love of our espousals is most likely to continue if we again and again begin where God began with us, and where we first began with God. It is wise to come to Him afresh, as we came in that first day when, helpless, needy, heavy-laden, we stood weeping at the cross and left our burden at the pierced feet. There we learned to look and live and love, and there would we repeat the lesson until we rehearse it perfectly in glory.

Tonight we have to talk about the love of God: "God so loved the world." That love of God is a very wonderful thing, especially when we see it set upon a lost, ruined, guilty world. What was there in the world that God should love it? There was nothing lovable in it. No fragrant flower grew in that arid desert. Enmity to Him, hatred to His truth, disregard of His law, rebellion against His commandments, those were the thorns and briars that covered the waste land. But no desirable thing blossomed there. Yet, "God loved the world," says the text. He "so" loved it, that even the writer of the book of John could not tell us how much. But so greatly, so divinely, did He love it that He gave His Son, His only Son, to redeem the world from perishing and to gather out of it a people to His praise.

Whence came that love? Not from anything outside of

God Himself. God's love springs from Himself. He loves because it is His nature to do so. "God is love." As I have said already, nothing upon the face of the earth could have merited His love, though there was much to merit His displeasure. This stream of love flows from its own secret source in the eternal Deity, and it owes nothing to any earth-born rain or rivulet. It springs from beneath the everlasting throne and fills itself full from the springs of the Infinite. God loved because He would love. When we inquire why the Lord loved this man or that, we have to come back to our Savior's answer to the question, "Even so, Father; for so it seemed good in thy sight" (Matt. 11:26). God has such love in His nature that He must needs let it flow forth to a world perishing by its own willful sin. When it flowed forth it was so deep, so wide, so strong that even inspiration could not compute its measure, and therefore the Holy Spirit gave us that great little word *so*, and left us to attempt the measurement, according as we perceive more and more of love divine.

Now, there happened to be an occasion upon which the great God could display His immeasurable love. The world had sadly gone astray. The world had lost itself. The world was tried and condemned. The world was given over to perish because of its offenses, and there was need for help. The fall of Adam and the destruction of humanity made ample room and verge enough for love almighty. Amid the ruins of humanity there was space for showing how much Jehovah loved the sons of men. For the compass of His love was no less than the world, the object of it no less than to deliver men from going down to the pit, and the result of it no less than the finding of a ransom for them. The far-reaching purpose of that love was both negative and positive—that, believing in Jesus, men might not perish, but have eternal life. The desperate disease of man gave occasion for the introduction of that divine remedy which God alone could have devised and supplied. By the plan of mercy, and the great gift that was needed for carrying it out, the Lord found means to display His boundless love to guilty men. Had there been no fall and no perishing, God might have shown His love to us as He does to the pure and perfect spirits that surround His throne. But He never could have commended His love to us to such an extent as He now does. In the gift of His only begotten Son, God commended His love to us, in that while we were yet sinners, in due time Christ died for the ungodly (see Rom. 5:8). The black background of sin makes the bright line of love shine out the more clearly. When the lightning writes the name of the Lord with flaming finger across the black brow of the tempest, we are compelled to see it. So when love inscribes the cross upon the jet tablet of our sin, even blind eyes must see that "herein is love" (1 John 4:10a).

I might handle my text in a thousand different ways tonight. But for simplicity's sake, and to keep to the one point of setting forth the love of God, I want to make you see how great that love is by five different particulars.

The Gift

The first is the *gift:* "God so loved the world, that *he gave his only begotten Son.*" Men who love much will give much, and you may usually measure the truth of love by its self-denials and sacrifices. That love which spares nothing, but spends itself to help and bless its object, is love indeed, and not the mere name of it. Little love forgets to bring water for the feet, but great love breaks its box of alabaster and lavishes its precious ointment (see Luke 7:36–50).

Consider, then, *what this gift was* that God gave. I should have to labor for expression if I were to attempt to set forth to the full this priceless boon. I will not court a failure by attempting the impossible. I will only invite you to think of the sacred Person whom the Great Father gave in order that He might prove His love to men. It was His only-begotten Son—His beloved Son—in whom He was well pleased. None of us had ever such a son to give. Ours are the sons of men; His was the Son of God. The Father gave His other self, one with Himself. When the great God gave His Son He gave God Himself, for Jesus is not in His eternal nature less than God. When God gave God for us He gave Himself. What more could He give? God gave His all—He gave Himself. Who can measure this love?

Judge, fathers, how you love your sons. Could you give them to die for your enemy? Judge, you who have an only son, how your hearts are entwined about your first-born, your only-begotten. There was no higher proof of Abraham's love to God than when he did not withhold from God his son, his only son, his Isaac whom he loved. There can certainly be no greater display of love than for the Eternal Father to give His only-begotten Son to die for us. No living thing will readily lose its offspring; man has peculiar grief when his son is taken. Has not God yet more?

A story has often been told of the fondness of parents for their children; how in a famine in the East a father and mother were reduced to absolute starvation, and the only possibility of preserving the life of the family was to sell one of the children into slavery. So they considered it. The pinch of hunger became unbearable, and their children pleading for bread tugged so painfully at their heartstrings, that they must entertain the idea of selling one to save the lives of the rest. They had four sons. Who of these should be sold? It must not be the first. How could they spare their first-born? The second was so strangely like his father that he seemed a reproduction of him, and the mother said that she would never part with *him*. The third was so singularly like the mother that the father said he would sooner die than that this dear boy should go into bondage. As for the fourth, he was their Benjamin, their last, their darling, and they could not part with *him*. They concluded that it were better for them all to die together than willingly to part with any one of their children. Do you not sympathize with them? I see you do. Yet God so loved us that, to put it very strongly, He seemed to love us better than His only Son and did not spare Him that He might spare us. He permitted His Son to perish from among men "that whosoever believeth in him should not perish, but have everlasting life."

If you desire to see the love of God in this great

procedure you must consider how He gave His Son. He did not give His Son, as you might do, to some profession in the pursuit of which you might still enjoy his company, but He gave His Son to exile among men. He sent Him down to yonder manger, united with a perfect humanity, which at the first was in an infant's form. There He slept where horned oxen fed! The Lord God sent the heir of all things to toil in a carpenter's shop—to drive the nail and push the plane and use the saw. He sent Him down among scribes and Pharisees, whose cunning eyes watched Him and whose cruel tongues scourged Him with base slanders. He sent Him down to hunger and thirst amid poverty so dire that He had no where to lay His head. He sent Him down to the scourging and the crowning with thorns, to the giving of His back to the smiters and His cheeks to those that plucked off the hair. At length He gave Him up to death—a felon's death, the death of the crucified. Behold that cross and see the anguish of Him who dies upon it. Mark how the Father has so given Him that He hides His face from Him and seems as if He would not own Him! *"Lama sabachthani"* tells us how fully God gave His Son to ransom the souls of the sinful. He gave Him to be made a curse for us, gave Him that He might die "the just for the unjust, that he might bring us to God" (1 Peter 3:18a).

Dear sirs, I can understand your giving up your children to go to India on her Majesty's service, or to go out to the Cameroons or the Congo upon the errands of our Lord Jesus. I can well comprehend your yielding them up even with the fear of a pestilential climate before you, for if they die they will die honorably in a glorious cause. But could you think of parting with them to die a felon's death upon a gibbet, execrated by those whom they sought to bless, stripped naked in body and deserted in mind? Would not that be too much? Would you not cry, "I cannot part with my son for such wretches as these. Why should he be put to a cruel death for such abominable beings, who even wash their hands in the blood of their best friend?" Remember that our Lord Jesus died what His countrymen considered to be an accursed death.

To the Romans it was the death of a condemned slave, a death that had all the elements of pain, disgrace, and scorn mingled in it to the uttermost. "But God commendeth his love toward us, in that, while we were yet sinners, Christ died for us" (Rom. 5:8). Oh, wondrous stretch of love, that Jesus Christ should die!

Yet, I cannot leave this point until I have you notice *when God gave His Son,* for there is love in the time. "God so loved the world, that he gave his only begotten Son." But when did He do that? In His eternal purpose He did this from before the foundation of the world. The words here used, "He gave his only begotten Son," cannot relate exclusively to the death of Christ, for Christ was not dead at the time of the utterance of this third chapter of John. Our Lord had just been speaking with Nicodemus, and that conversation took place at the beginning of His ministry. The fact is that Jesus was always the gift of God. The promise of Jesus was made in the garden of Eden almost as soon as Adam fell. On the spot where our ruin was accomplished, a Deliverer was bestowed whose heel should be bruised, but who should break the serpent's head beneath His foot.

Throughout the ages the great Father stood to His gift. He looked upon His only begotten as man's hope, the inheritance of the chosen seed, who in Him would possess all things. Every sacrifice was God's renewal of His gift of grace, a reassurance that He had bestowed the gift and would never draw back therefrom. The whole system of types under the law betokened that in the fullness of time the Lord would in very deed give up His Son, to be born of a woman, to bear the iniquities of His people, and to die the death in their behalf. I greatly admire this pertinacity of love. For many a man in a moment of generous excitement can perform a supreme act of benevolence, and yet could not bear to look at it calmly and consider it from year to year. The slow fire of anticipation would have been unbearable. If the Lord should take away yonder dear boy from his mother, she would bear the blow with some measure of patience, heavy as it would be to her tender heart. But suppose that she were credibly informed that on such a day her boy must die, and thus had from year to year to look upon him as one dead, would it not cast a cloud over every hour of her future life? Suppose also that she knew that he would be hanged upon a tree to die, as one condemned. Would it not embitter her existence? If she could withdraw from such a trial, would she not? Assuredly she would. Yet the Lord God spared not His own Son, but freely delivered Him up for us all, doing it in His heart from age to age. Herein is love—love which many waters could not quench; love eternal, inconceivable, infinite!

Now, as this gift refers not only to our Lord's death, but to the ages before it, so it includes also all the ages afterward. God "so loved the world that he gave"—and still gives—"his only begotten Son, that whosoever believeth in him should not perish, but have everlasting life." The Lord is giving Christ away tonight. Oh, that thousands of you may gladly accept the gift unspeakable! Will anyone refuse? This good gift, this perfect gift—can you decline it? Oh, that you may have faith to lay hold on Jesus, for thus He will be yours. He is God's free gift to all free receivers, a full Christ for empty sinners. If you can but hold out your empty willing hand, the Lord will give Christ to you at this moment. Nothing is freer than a gift. Nothing is more worth having than a gift that comes fresh from the hand of God, as full of effectual power as ever it was. The fountain is eternal, but the stream from it is as fresh as when first the fountain was open. There is no exhausting this gift.

> Dear dying Lamb, thy precious blood
>   Shall never lose its power
> Until all the ransomed church of God
>   Be saved to sin no more.

See, then, what is the love of God, that He gave His Son from of old and has never revoked the gift. He stands to His gift and continues still to give His dear Son to all who are willing to accept Him. Out of the riches of His grace He has given, is giving, and will give the Lord Jesus

Christ, and all the priceless gifts that are contained in Him, to all needy sinners who will simply trust Him.

I call upon you from this first point to admire the love of God because of the transcendent greatness of His gift to the world, even the gift of His only begotten Son.

The Plan of Salvation

Now notice secondly, and, I think I may say, with equal admiration, the love of God in *the plan of salvation*. He has put it thus: "that whosoever believeth in him should not perish, but have everlasting life." The way of salvation is extremely simple to understand and exceedingly easy to practice when once the heart is made willing and obedient. The method of the covenant of grace differs as much from that of the covenant of works as light from darkness. It is not said that God has given His Son to all who will keep His law, for that we could not do, and therefore the gift would have been available to none of us. Nor is it said that He has given His Son to all that experience terrible despair and bitter remorse, for that is not felt by many who nevertheless are the Lord's own people. But the great God has given His own Son, that "whosoever believeth in him" should not perish. Faith, however slender, saves the soul. Trust in Christ is the certain way of eternal happiness.

Now, what is it to believe in Jesus? It is just this: It is to trust yourself with Him. If your hearts are ready, though you have never believed in Jesus before, I trust you will believe in Him now. O Holy Spirit, graciously make it so.

What is it to believe in Jesus?

It is, first, to give your *firm and cordial assent* to the truth that God did send His Son, born of a woman, to stand in the room and stead of guilty men. To believe that God did cause to meet on Him the iniquities of us all, so that He bore the punishment due to our transgressions, being made a curse for us. We must heartily believe the Scripture that says: "the chastisement of our peace was upon him, and with his stripes we are healed" (Isa. 53:5). I ask for our assent to the grand doctrine of substitution, which is the marrow of the Gospel. Oh, may God the Holy Spirit lead you to give a cordial assent to it at once. For wonderful as it is, it is a fact that God was in Christ reconciling the world to Himself, not imputing their trespasses to them. Oh that you may rejoice that this is true, and be thankful that such a blessed fact is revealed by God Himself. Believe that the substitution of the Son of God is certain. Cavil not at the plan, nor question its validity, or efficacy, as many do.

Alas! they kick at God's great sacrifice and count it a sorry invention. As for me, since God has ordained to save man by a substitutionary sacrifice, I joyfully agree to His method and see no reason to do anything else but admire it and adore the Author of it. I joy and rejoice that such a plan should have been thought of, whereby the justice of God is vindicated, and His mercy is set free to do all that He desires. Sin is punished in the person of the Christ, yet mercy is extended to the guilty. In Christ mercy is sustained by justice, and justice satisfied by an act of mercy. The worldly wise say hard things about this device of infinite wisdom. But as for me, I love the very name of the cross and count it to be the center of wisdom, the focus of love, the heart of righteousness. This is a main point of faith—to give a hearty assent to the giving of Jesus to suffer in our place and stead, to agree with all our soul and mind to this way of salvation.

The second thing is that you do *accept this for yourself.* In Adam's sin, you did not sin personally, for you were not then in existence—yet you fell. Neither can you now complain thereof, for you have willingly endorsed and adopted Adam's sin by committing personal transgressions. You have laid your hand, as it were, upon Adam's sin and made it your own by committing personal and actual sin. Thus you perished by the sin of another, which you adopted and endorsed. In like manner must you be saved by the righteousness of another, which you are to accept and appropriate. Jesus has offered an atonement, and that atonement becomes yours when you accept it by putting your trust in Him. I want you now to say,

My faith doth lay her hand
On that dear head of thine
While, like a penitent, I stand,
And here confess my sin.

Surely this is no very difficult matter. To say that Christ who hung upon the cross shall be my Christ, my surety, needs neither stretch of intellect, nor splendor of character; yet it is the act that brings salvation to the soul.

One thing more is needful, and that is *personal trust.* First comes assent to the truth, then acceptance of that truth for yourself, and then a simple trusting of yourself wholly to Christ as a substitute. The essence of faith is trust, reliance, dependence. Fling away every other confidence of every sort, save confidence in Jesus. Do not allow a ghost of a shade of a shadow of a confidence in anything that you can do, or in anything that you can be. But look alone to Him whom God has set forth to be the propitiation for sin. This I do at this very moment. Will you not do the same? Oh, may the sweet Spirit of God lead you now to trust in Jesus!

See, then, the love of God in putting it in so plain, so easy a way. Oh, broken, crushed, and despairing sinner, you cannot work, but can you not believe that which is true? You cannot sigh, you cannot cry, you cannot melt your stony heart. But can you not believe that Jesus died for you, and that He can change that heart of yours and make you a new creature? If you can believe this, then trust in Jesus to do so, and you are saved, for he that believes in Him is justified. "He that believeth on the Son *hath* everlasting life" (John 3:36a). He is a saved man. His sins are forgiven him. Let him go his way in peace and sin no more.

I admire, first, the love of God in the great gift, and then in the great plan by which that gift becomes available to guilty men.

The Persons for Whom This Plan Is Available

The love of God shines forth with transcendent brightness in a third point, namely, in *the persons for whom this plan is available,* and for whom this gift is given. They are described in these words—"Whosoever believeth in him." There is in the text a word that has no limit—"God so loved the world." But then comes in the descriptive limit, which I beg you to notice with care: "He gave his only begotten Son, *that whosoever believeth in him* should not perish." God did not so love the world that any man who does not believe in Christ shall be saved; neither did God so give His Son that any man shall be saved who refuses to believe in Him. See how it is put—"God so loved the world, that he gave his only begotten Son, that whosoever believeth in him should not perish." Here is the compass of the love: While every unbeliever is excluded, every believer is included. "Whosoever believeth in him."

Suppose there be a man who has been guilty of all the lusts of the flesh to an infamous degree. Suppose that he is so detestable that he is only fit to be treated like a moral leper and shut up in a separate house for fear he would contaminate those who hear or see him. Yet if that man shall believe in Jesus Christ, he shall at once be made clean from his defilement and shall not perish because of his sin. And suppose there be another man who, in the pursuit of his selfish motives, has ground down the poor, has robbed his fellow-traders, and has even gone so far as to commit actual crime of which the law has taken cognizance, yet if he believes in the Lord Jesus Christ he shall be led to make restitution, and his sins shall be forgiven him.

I once heard of a preacher addressing a company of men in chains condemned to die for murder and other crimes. They were such a drove of beasts to all outward appearances that it seemed hopeless to preach to them. Yet were I set to be chaplain to such a wretched company I should not hesitate to tell them that "God so loved the world, that he gave his only begotten Son, that whosoever believeth in him should not perish, but have everlasting life." O man, if you will believe in Jesus as the Christ, however horrible your past sins have been, they shall be blotted out. You shall be saved from the power of your evil habits, and you shall begin again like a new-born child with a new and true life, which God shall give you. "Whosoever believeth in him"—that takes you in, my aged friend, now lingering within a few tottering steps of the grave. O gray-headed sinner, if you believe in Him, you shall not perish. The text also includes you, dear boy, who has scarcely entered your teens as yet. If you believe in Him, you shall not perish. That takes you in, fair maiden, and gives you hope and joy while yet young. That comprehends all of us, provided we believe in the Lord Jesus Christ.

Neither can all the devils in hell find out any reason why the man that believes in Christ shall be lost, for it is written, "Him that cometh to me I will in no wise cast out" (John 6:37b). Do they say, "Lord, he has been so long in coming"? The Lord replies, "Has he come? Then I will not cast him out for all his delays." "But, Lord, he went back after making a profession." "Has he at length come? Then I will not cast him out for all his backslidings." "But, Lord, he was a foul-mouthed blasphemer." "Has he come to me? Then I will not cast him out for all his blasphemies." "But," says one, "I take exception to the salvation of this wicked wretch. He has behaved so abominably that in all justice he ought to be sent to hell." Just so. But if he repents of his sin and believes in the Lord Jesus Christ, whoever he may be, he shall not be sent there. He shall be changed in character, so that he shall never perish but have eternal life.

Now, observe, that this "whosoever" makes a grand sweep, for it encircles all degrees of faith. "Whosoever believeth in him." It may be that he has no full assurance. It may be that he has no assurance at all. But if he has faith, true and childlike, by it he shall be saved. Though his faith be so little that I must needs put on my spectacles to see it, yet Christ will see it and reward it. His faith is such a tiny grain of mustard seed that I look and look again but hardly discern it, and yet it brings him eternal life. It is itself a living thing. The Lord can see within that mustard seed a tree among whose branches the birds of the air shall make their nests.

> My faith is feeble, I confess,
> I faintly trust thy word;
> But wilt thou pity me the less?
> Be that far from thee, Lord!

O Lord Jesus, if I cannot take You up in my arms as Simeon did, I will at least touch Your garment's hem as the poor diseased woman did, to whom Your healing virtue flowed. It is written, "God so loved the world, that he gave his only begotten Son, that whosoever believeth in him should not perish, but have everlasting life." That means me. I cannot preach at length to you tonight, but I would preach with strength. Oh that this truth may soak into your souls. Oh you that feel yourselves guilty, and you that feel guilty because you do not feel guilty— you that are broken in heart because your heart will not break, you that feel that you cannot feel—it is to you that I would preach salvation in Christ by faith. You groan because you cannot groan. But whoever you may be, you are still within the range of this mighty word, that "whosoever believeth in him should not perish, but have everlasting life."

Thus have I commended God's love to you in those three points—the divine gift, the divine method of saving, and the divine choice of the persons to whom salvation comes.

The Deliverance

Now fourthly, another beam of divine love is to be seen in the negative blessing here stated, namely, in *the deliverance* implied in the words, "that whosoever believeth in him should *not perish*."

I understand that word to mean that whosoever believes in the Lord Jesus Christ shall not perish, though he is ready to perish. His sins would cause him to perish, but he shall never perish. At first he has a little hope in Christ, but its existence is feeble. It will soon die out, will it not? No, his faith shall not perish, for this promise covers it—"Whosoever believeth in him should not perish." The penitent has believed in Jesus, and therefore he has begun to be a Christian. "Oh," cries an enemy, "let him alone. He will soon be back among us. He will soon be as careless as ever." Listen, "Whosoever believeth in him should not perish," and therefore he will not return to his former state.

This proves the final perseverance of the saints, for if the believer ceased to be a believer he would perish. As he cannot perish, it is clear that he will continue a believer. If you believe in Jesus, you shall never leave off believing in Him, for that would be to perish. If you believe in Him, you shall never delight in your old sins, for that would be to perish. If you believe in Him, you shall never lose spiritual life. How can you lose that which is everlasting? If you were to lose it, it would prove that it was not everlasting, and you would perish. Thus you would make this word to be of no effect. Whosoever with his heart believes in Christ is a saved man, not for tonight only, but for all the nights that ever shall be and for that dread night of death and for that solemn eternity that draws so near. "Whosoever believeth in him should not perish," but he shall have a life that cannot die, a justification that cannot be disputed, an acceptance that shall never cease.

What is it to perish? It is to lose all hope in Christ, all trust in God, all light in life, all peace in death, all joy, all bliss, all union with God. This shall never happen to you if you believe in Christ. If you believe, you shall be chastened when you do wrong, for every child of God comes under discipline. What son is there whom the Father chastens not? If you believe, you may doubt and fear as to your state, as a man on board a ship may be tossed about, but you have gotten on board a ship that never can be wrecked. He that has union with Christ has union with perfection, omnipotence, and glory. He that believes is a member of Christ. Will Christ lose His members? How would Christ be perfect if He lost even His little finger? Are Christ's members to rot off, or to be cut off? Impossible. If you have faith in Christ, you are a partaker of Christ's life, and you cannot perish. If men were trying to drown me, they could not drown my foot as long as I had my head above water. As long as our Head is above water up yonder in the eternal sunshine, the least limb of His body can never be destroyed. He that believes in Jesus is united to Him, and he must live because Jesus lives. Oh, what a word is this, "I give unto [my sheep] eternal life; and they shall never perish, neither shall any man pluck them out of my hand. My Father, which gave them me, is greater than all; and no man is able to pluck them out of my Father's hand" (John 10:28–29).

I feel that I have a grand Gospel to preach to you when I read that whosoever believes in Jesus shall not perish. I would not give two pins for that trumpery, temporary salvation that some proclaim, which floats the soul for a time and then ebbs away to apostasy. I do not believe that the man who is once in Christ may live in sin and delight in it, and yet be saved. That is abominable teaching, and none of mine. But I believe that the man who is in Christ will *not* live in sin, for he is saved from it; nor will he return to his old sins and abide in them, for the grace of God will continue to save him from his sins. Such a change is wrought by regeneration that the newborn man cannot abide in sin, nor find comfort in it, but he loves holiness and makes progress in it.

The Ethiopian may change his skin, and the leopard his spots (Jer. 13:23), but only grace divine can work the change. It would be as great a miracle to undo the work of God as to do it. To destroy the new creation would require as great a power as to make it. As only God can create, so only God can destroy. He will never destroy the work of His own hands. Will God begin to build and not finish? Will He commence a warfare and end it before He has won the victory? What would the Devil say if Christ were to begin to save a soul and fail in the attempt? If there should come to be souls in hell that were believers in Christ, and yet did perish, it would cast a cloud upon the diadem of our exalted Lord. It cannot, shall not, be. Such is the love of God, that whosoever believes in His dear Son shall not perish. In this assurance we greatly rejoice.

The Possession

The last commendation of His love lies in *the positive—in the possession*. I shall have to go in a measure over the same ground again. Let me therefore be the shorter. God gives to every man that believes in Christ everlasting life. The moment you believe there trembles into your bosom a vital spark of heavenly flame that never shall be quenched. In that same moment when you cast yourself on Christ, Christ comes to you in the living and incorruptible Word that lives and abides forever. Though there should drop into your heart but one drop of the heavenly water of life, remember this: He has said it who cannot lie. "The water that I shall give him shall be in him a well of water springing up into everlasting life" (John 4:14b).

When I first received everlasting life I had no idea what a treasure had come to me. I knew that I had obtained something very extraordinary, but of its superlative value I was not aware. I did but look to Christ in the little chapel, and I received eternal life. I looked to Jesus, He looked on me, and we were one forever. That moment my joy surpassed all bounds, just as my sorrow had aforetime driven me to an extreme of grief. I was perfectly at rest in Christ, satisfied with Him, and my heart was glad. But I did not know that this grace was everlasting life until I began to read in the Scriptures, and to know more fully the value of the jewel that God had given me.

The next Sunday I went to the same chapel, as it was very natural that I should. But I never went afterward, for this reason, that during my first week the new life that was in me had been compelled to fight for its existence, and a conflict with the old nature had been vigorously carried on. This I knew to be a special token of the indwelling of grace in my soul. But in that same chapel I heard a sermon upon "O wretched man that I am! who shall deliver me from the body of this death?" (Rom. 7:24). And the preacher declared that Paul was not a Christian when he had that experience. Babe as I was, I knew better than to believe so absurd a statement. What but divine grace could produce such a sighing and crying after deliverance from indwelling sin? I felt that a person who could talk such nonsense knew little of the life of a true believer. I said to myself, "What! Am I not alive because I feel a conflict within me? I never felt this fight when I was an unbeliever. When I was not a Christian I never groaned to be set free from sin. This conflict is one of the surest evidences of my new birth, and yet this man cannot see it. He may be a good exhorter to sinners, but he cannot feed believers." I resolved to go into that pasture no more, for I could not feed therein. I find that the struggle becomes more and more intense. Each victory over sin reveals another army of evil tendencies, and I am never able to sheathe my sword, nor cease from prayer and watchfulness.

I cannot advance an inch without praying my way, nor keep the inch I gain without watching and standing fast. Grace alone can preserve and perfect me. The old nature will kill the new nature if it can, and to this moment the only reason why my new nature is not dead is this—because it cannot die. If it could have died, it would have been slain long ago. But Jesus said, "I give unto [my sheep] eternal life" (John 10:28a). "He that believeth on [me] hath everlasting life" (John 3:36a), and therefore, the believer cannot die. The only religion that will save you is one that you cannot leave because it possesses you and will not leave you.

If you hold a doctrine that you can give up, give it up. But if the doctrines are burned into you so that as long as you live you must hold them, and so that if you were burned every ash would hold that same truth in it because you are impregnated with it, then you have found the right thing. You are not a saved man unless Christ has saved you forever. But that which has such a grip on you that its grasp is felt in the core of your being is the power of God. To have Christ living in you, and the truth ingrained in your very nature—O people, *this* is the thing that saves the soul, and nothing short of it.

It is written in the text, "God so loved the world, that he gave his only begotten Son, that whosoever believeth in him should not perish, but have everlasting life." What is this but a life that shall last through your thirty years, a life that shall last you should you outlive a century? Is it a life that will still flourish when you lie at the grave's mouth, a life that will abide when you have quitted the body and left it rotting in the tomb? Is it a life that will continue when your body is raised again, and you shall stand before the judgment seat of Christ? Is it a life that will outshine those stars and the sun and the moon, a life that shall be coeval with the life of the Eternal Father? As long as there is a God, the believer shall not only exist, but live. As long as there is a heaven, you shall enjoy it. As long as there is a Christ, you shall live in His love. And as long as there is an eternity, you shall continue to fill it with delight.

God bless you and help you to believe in Jesus. Amen.

The Perfect Love of God to Us

Robert Murray McCheyne (1813–1843) is one of the brightest lights of the Church of Scotland. Born in Dundee, he was educated in Edinburgh and licensed to preach in 1835. For a brief time, he assisted his friend Andrew A. Bonar at Larbert and Dunipace. In 1836 he was ordained and installed as pastor of Saint Peter's Church, Dundee, where he served until his untimely death two months short of his thirtieth birthday. He was known for his personal sanctity and his penetrating ministry of the Word, and great crowds came to hear him preach. *The Memoirs of and Remains of Robert Murray McCheyne,* edited by Andrew Bonar, is a Christian classic that every minister of the Gospel should read.

This sermon, preached in 1842, was taken from *The Memoirs of and Remains of Robert Murray McCheyne,* edited by Andrew Bonar and published in 1872 by William Oliphant, Edinburgh.

4

THE PERFECT LOVE
OF GOD TO US

There is no fear in love; but perfect love casteth out fear: because fear hath torment. He that feareth is not made perfect in love. We love him, because he first loved us. If a man say, I love God, and hateth his brother, he is a liar: for he that loveth not his brother whom he hath seen, how can he love God whom he hath not seen? And this commandment have we from him, That he who loveth God love his brother also (1 John 4:18–21).

DOCTRINE—"perfect love casteth out fear."

The State of an Awakened Soul—
"Fear Hath Torment"

There are two kinds of fear mentioned in the Bible very opposite from one another. The one is the very atmosphere of heaven, the other is the very atmosphere of hell.

There is the fear of love. This is the very temper of a little child: "The fear of the LORD is the beginning of wisdom" (Prov. 9:10a). This was the mind of Job. He "feared God and eschewed evil" (Job 1:1). No, it is the very Spirit of the Lord Jesus. On Him rested "the spirit . . . of the fear of the LORD; and [made] him of quick understanding in the fear of the LORD" (Isa. 11:2–3).

There is the fear of terror. This is the very temper of devils: "The devils also believe, and tremble" (James 2:19b). This is what was in Adam and Eve after the Fall. They fled from the voice of God and tried to hide themselves in one of the trees of the garden. This was the state of the jailer when he trembled and sprang in and brought them out and fell at their feet, saying, "Sirs, what must I do to be saved?" (Acts 16:30). This is the fear here spoken of—tormenting fear. "Fear hath torment." Some of you have felt this fear that has torment. Many more might feel it this day; you are within reach of it. Let me explain its rise in the soul.

A natural man casts off fear and restrains prayer before God. "[They] hath been at ease from [their] youth, and . . . settled on [their] lees, and hath not been emptied from vessel to vessel, . . . therefore, [their] taste remained in [them], and [their] scent is not changed" (Jer. 48:11). They are like fallow ground that has never been broken up by the plow but is overrun with briers and thorns. Are there not some among you that never trembled for your soul? You think you are as good as your neighbors. Ah! well, your dream will be broken up one day soon.

When the Spirit of God opens the eyes, He makes the stoutest sinner tremble. He shows him *the number of his sins,* or rather that they cannot be numbered. Before, he had a memory that easily forgot his sins. Oaths slipped over his tongue, and he knew it not. Every day added new sins to his page on God's book, yet he remembered not. But now the Spirit of God sets all his sins straight before him. All unpardoned, long-forgotten enormities rise up behind him. Then he begins to tremble. "Innumerable evils have compassed me about" (Ps. 40:12).

The Spirit makes him feel the greatness of sin, the exceeding sinfulness of it. Before, it seemed nothing. But now, it rises like a flood over the soul. The wrath of God he feels abiding on him; a terrible sound is in his ears. He knows not what to do. His fear has torment. Sin is seen now as done against a holy God, done against a God of love, done against Jesus Christ and His love.

A fourth thing that awfully torments the soul is corruption working in the heart. Often persons under conviction are made to feel the awful workings of corruption in their heart. Often temptation and conviction of sin meet together and awfully torment the soul, rending it into pieces. Conviction of sin is piercing his heart, driving him to flee from the wrath to come. Yet at the same moment some raging lust, or envy, or horrid malice is boiling in his heart, driving him toward hell. Then a man feels a hell within him. In hell there will be this awful mixture: There will be an overwhelming dread of the wrath of God, and yet corruption, boiling up within, will drive the soul more and more into the flames. This is often felt on earth. Some of you may be feeling it. This is the fear that has torment.

Another thing the Spirit convinces the soul of is the inability to help oneself. When a man is first awakened, he says, "I shall soon get myself out of this sad condition." He falls upon many contrivances to justify himself. He changes his life. He tries to repent, to pray. He is soon taught that his "righteousnesses are as filthy rags" (Isa. 64:6)—that he is trying to cover rags with filthy rags. He is brought to feel that all he can do signifies just nothing, and that he never can bring a clean thing out of an unclean thing. This sinks the soul in gloom. This fear has torment.

He fears he shall never be in Christ. Some of you perhaps know that this fear has torment. The free offer of Christ is the very thing that pierces you to the heart. You hear that He is altogether lovely—that He invites sinners to come to Him—that He never casts out those that do come. But you fear you will never be one of these. You fear you have sinned too long or too much—you have sinned away your day of grace. Ah! this fear has torment.

Some will say, "It is not good to be awakened, then."

It is the way to peace that passes understanding. It is God's chosen method to bring you to feel your need of Christ before you come to Christ. At present your peace is like a dream! When you awake you will find it so. Ask awakened souls if they would go back again to their slumber. Ah, no! If I die, let me die at the foot of the cross; let me not perish unawakened.

You must be awakened one day. If not now, you will afterward in hell. After death, fear will come on your secure souls. There is not one unawakened soul in hell; all are trembling there. The devils tremble, the damned spirits tremble. Would it not be better to tremble now and flee to Jesus Christ for refuge? *Now,* He is waiting to be gracious to you. *Then,* He will mock when your fear comes. You will know through all eternity that "fear hath torment."

The Change on Believing—"There Is No Fear in Love, but Perfect Love Casteth Out Fear"

The love here spoken of is not our love to God, but *His love to us,* for it is called perfect love. All that is ours is imperfect. When we have done all, we must say, "We are unprofitable servants" (Luke 17:10). Sin mingles with all we think and do. It was no comfort to tell us that if we would love God perfectly it would cast out fear. For how can we work that love into our souls? It is the Father's love to us that casts out fear. He is *the Perfect One.* All His works are perfect. He can do nothing but what is perfect. His knowledge is perfect knowledge; His wrath is perfect wrath; His love is *perfect love.* It is this perfect love that casts out fear. Just as the sunbeams cast out darkness wherever they fall, so does this love cast out fear.

But where does this love fall? It falls on Jesus Christ. Twice God spoke from heaven and said, "This is my beloved Son, in whom I am well pleased" (Matt. 3:17; 17:5). God perfectly loves His own Son. He sees infinite beauty in His person. God sees Himself manifested. He is infinitely pleased with His finished work. The infinite heart of the infinite God flows out in love toward our Lord Jesus Christ. And there is no fear in the bosom of Christ. All His fears are past. Once He said, "While I suffer thy terrors I am distracted" (Ps. 88:15). But now He is in perfect love, and perfect love casts out fear.

Hearken, trembling souls! Here you may find rest to your souls. You do not need to live another hour under your tormenting fears. Jesus Christ has borne the wrath of which you are afraid. He now stands a refuge for the oppressed—a refuge in the time of trouble. Look to Christ and your fear will be cast out. Come to the feet of Christ and you will find rest. Call upon the name of the Lord and you will be delivered. You say you cannot look, nor come, nor cry, for you are helpless. Hear, then, and your soul shall live. Jesus is a Savior to the helpless. Christ is not only a Savior to those who are naked and empty, and have no goodness to recommend themselves, but He is a Savior to those who are unable to give themselves to Him. You cannot be in too desperate a condition for Christ. As long as you remain unbelieving, you are under His perfect wrath—wrath without any mixture. The wrath of God will be as amazing as His love. It comes out of the same bosom. But the moment you look to Christ, you will come under His perfect love—love without any coldness—light without any shade—love without any cloud or mountain between. God's love will cast out all your fears.

His Love Gives Boldness in the Day of Judgment

"Herein is our love made perfect, that we may have boldness in the day of judgment: because as he is, so are we in this world" (1 John 4:17). There is a great day coming, often spoken of in the Bible—the day of judgment—the day when God shall judge the secrets of men's hearts by Christ Jesus. The Christless will not be able to stand in that day. The ungodly shall not stand in the judgment. At present, sinners have much boldness; their neck is an iron sinew and their brow brass. Many of them cannot blush when they are caught in sin. Among ourselves, is it not amazing how bold sinners are in forsaking ordinances? With what a brazen face will some men swear! How bold some ungodly men are in coming to the Lord's table! But it will not be so in a little while. When Christ shall appear—the holy Jesus, in all His glory—then brazen-faced sinners will begin to blush. Those that never prayed will begin to wail. Sinners, whose limbs carried them stoutly to sin and to the Lord's table last Sunday, will find their knees knocking against one another.

Who shall abide the day of His coming, and who shall stand when He appears (see Mal. 3:2)? When the books are opened—the one, the book of God's remembrance, the other the Bible—then the dead will be judged out of those things written in the books. Then the heart of the ungodly will die within them; then will begin their "shame and everlasting contempt" (Dan. 12:2). Many wicked persons comfort themselves with this, that their sin is not known—that no eye sees them. But in that day the most secret sins will be all brought out to the light. "Every idle word that men shall speak, they shall give account thereof in the day of judgment" (Matt. 12:36). How would you tremble and blush, O wicked man, if I were now to go over before this congregation the secret sins you have committed during the past week—all your secret fraud and cheating, your secret uncleanness, your secret malice and envy—how you would blush and be confounded! How much more in that day, when the secrets of your whole life shall be made manifest before an assembled world! What eternal confusion will sink down your soul in that day! You will be quite chopfallen. All your pride and blustering will be gone.

All in Christ will have boldness—

Because Christ shall be Judge. What abundant peace will it give you in that day, believer, when you see Christ is Judge! He that shed His blood for you—He that is your Surety, your Shepherd, your all, He will be Judge. It will take away all fear. You will be able to say, "Who shall condemn? For Christ has died." In the very hand that opens the books you will see the marks of the wounds made by your sins. Christ will be the same to you in the judgment that He is now.

Because the Father Himself loves you. Christ and the Father are one. The Father sees no sin in you because, as Christ is, so are you in this world. You are judged by God according to what the Surety is, so that God's love will be with you in that day. You will feel the smile of the Father, and you will bear the voice of Jesus saying, "Come, ye blessed of my Father" (Matt. 25:34).

Learn to fear nothing between this and judgment. Fear not—wait on the Lord and be of good courage.

The Consequences of Being in the Love of God

"We love him, because he first loved us" (1 John 4:19). When a poor sinner cleaves to Jesus and finds the forgiving love of God, he cannot but love God back again. When the prodigal returned home and felt his father's arms around his neck, then did he feel the gushings of affection toward his father. When the summer sun shines

full down upon the sea, it draws the vapors upward to the sky. So when the sunbeams of the Sun of Righteousness fall upon the soul, they draw forth the constant risings of love to Him in return.

Some of you are longing to be able to love God. Come into His love, then. Consent to be loved by Him, though worthless in yourself. It is better to be loved by Him than to love, and it is the only way to learn to love Him. When the light of the sun falls upon the moon, it finds the moon dark and unlovely. But the moon reflects the light and casts it back again. So let the love of God shine into your breast, and you will cast it back again. The love of Christ constrains us. "We love him, because he first loved us." The only cure for a cold heart is to look at the heart of Jesus.

Some of you give no love to God because you love an idol. You may be sure you have never come into His love—that curse rests upon you: "If any man love not the Lord Jesus Christ, let him be Anathema Maranatha" (1 Cor. 16:22).

We love our brother also (see 1 John 4:21). If you love an absent person, you will love their picture. What is that the sailor's wife keeps so closely wrapped in a napkin, laid up in her best drawer among sweet-smelling flowers? She takes it out morning and evening, and gazes at it through her tears. It is the picture of her absent husband. She loves it because it is like him. It has many imperfections, but still it is like him. Believers are the pictures of God in this world. The Spirit of Christ dwells in them. They walk as He walked. True, they are full of imperfections, still they are true copies. If you love Him, you will love them. You will make them your bosom friends.

Are there none of you that dislike real Christians? You do not like their look, their ways, their speech, their prayers. You call them hypocrites and keep away from them. Do you know the reason? You hate the copy because you hate the original. You hate Christ and are none of His.

The Keynote of the Bible

Reuben Archer Torrey (1856–1928) was one of America's best-known evangelists and Bible teachers. Educated at Yale and various German universities, he went through a time of skepticism from which he emerged a staunch preacher of the faith. In 1889, D. L. Moody called Torrey from the pastorate to become superintendent of his new school in Chicago, now the Moody Bible Institute. He also served as pastor of the Chicago Avenue Church, now the Moody Church. He and Charles Alexander conducted evangelistic meetings together in many parts of the world. From 1912–19, Torrey served as dean of the Bible Institute of Los Angeles. He served from 1914 as pastor of the Church of the Open Door. From 1924 to his death, he ministered in conferences and taught at the Moody Bible Institute.

This sermon was taken from his book *The Gospel for Today,* published in 1922 by Fleming H. Revell Co.

Reuben Archer Torrey

5

THE KEYNOTE OF THE BIBLE

God is love (1 John 4:8b ASV).

OUR SUBJECT IS, "The keynote of the Bible." You will find the keynote of the Bible in 1 John 4:8, "God is love." That is one of the shortest sentences ever written, and it is certainly one of the greatest and most profound. It is inexhaustible in its meaning and in its scope. Men have been studying, scrutinizing, pondering, and digging into that sentence through the eighteen centuries that have passed since it was written, and they have not exhausted it yet. Thousands upon thousands of sermons have been preached upon that text, yet something new awaits it and seeks to expound it. Thousands of volumes have been written by some of the world's greatest thinkers, devoted to the study, exposition, and application of that sentence, but it is as fresh and full as ever. It is constantly yielding new treasures to each new century and to each new explorer of its exhaustless wealth. Men and angels will ponder that sentence throughout the endless ages of eternity and not exhaust it.

The Book that contains that matchless sentence bears the unmistakable seal of having God for its Author. The golden truth of priceless worth contained in this sentence is peculiar to the Bible. All the philosophers in the world never discovered that stupendous truth until God revealed it and the Bible declared it. The world would never have known that "God is love," had not God revealed the fact in His own Word. It is true that there are evidences of beneficent design in nature and in history, but nature and history have both been marred by Satan's work and by the entrance of sin into the world. It is only that interpretation of history and that insight into the future of man and nature and Satan that the Bible gives that enables us to see love reigning above all and through all.

We hear much in these days of the profound truths contained in the teachings of the world's great philosophers of ancient and of modern times, in philosophers like Socrates, Plato, Aristotle, Seneca, Isocrates, Epictetus, Marcus Aurelius Antoninus, and in the teachings of the great founders of religions like Buddha, Mohammed, Confucius, and Zoroaster. But in none of them do we find this great truth that "God is love," nor anything akin to it, not until the Bible revealed it. We owe this truth wholly and solely to the Bible. We must go then to the Bible for the interpretation of this truth.

This sentence is the keynote of the entire Bible. It is the great fundamental thought of the Bible. If anyone were to ask me to put into one sentence what the Bible teaches, I could do it. And this would be the sentence, "God is love." From start to finish, from Genesis 1:1 to Revelation 22:21, the Bible is one great, ever-swelling anthem, and the theme of that anthem is, "God is love." God's love is the keynote of the whole Bible, of each one of the sixty-six books that go to make up the completed whole. It was the love of God that led to the Creation as described in the first chapter of Genesis. It was God's love that led to the banishment of Adam and Eve from the Garden of Eden when they fell as recorded in the third chapter of Genesis. It was God's love that led to the promise of the Savior, the seed of the woman, immediately after Adam and Eve had fallen. It was God's love that led to the call of Abraham, Isaac, and Jacob to be a blessing first to their own descendants and ultimately to the whole human race. It was God's love that led to the bondage of Israel in Egypt and to their deliverance from that bondage when the time was ripe. It was God's love that led to the giving of the law through Moses on Sinai, and it was God's love that led to the extermination of the Canaanites.

It was God's love that led to the planting of Israel in that land so wondrously adapted by its natural configuration and by its location in the then inhabited world to be the training place of the nation that would bring blessing to the whole earth, and from which the Savior would be born. It was God's love that shaped Israel's history through all their wanderings from Him. It was God's love that at last rooted Israel out of "the land" He had given them and scattered them through the earth. It will be God's love that restores them again to "the land" that belongs to them by eternal covenant when the time is full. It was God's love that sent Jesus Christ to die for sinful men, to rise again from the dead, and to ascend to the right hand of the Father in the glory. And it will be God's love that will send Him back again to earth when the fullness of time for that greatest event in all this earth's history has come. Heaven and all its glories, hell and all its horrors, both have their origin in the love of God. Yes, "God is love," is the keynote of the Bible, the secret of history, the explanation of nature, and the solution of eternity's mysteries.

I wish to call your attention to some of the ways in which the love of God is manifested. Of course, it would take many sermons to recount all the manifestations of the love of God, but we can look at some of them though it would take all eternity to fully understand and appreciate even them.

God's Love Manifests Itself in His Ministering to Our Needs and Joy

In the first place, *God's love manifests itself in His ministering to all our needs and to our fullest joy*. This comes out again and again in the Bible. For example, our Lord Jesus in expounding to His disciples their own duty says in Matthew 5:44–45, "Love your enemies, and pray for them that persecute you; that ye may be sons of your Father who is in heaven: for he maketh his sun to rise on the evil and on the good, and sendeth rain on the just and on the unjust." And way back in the Old Testament in Deuteronomy 32:9–12 we read, "For Jehovah's portion is his people; Jacob is the lot of his inheritance. He found him in a desert land, and in the waste, howling wilderness; he led him about, he instructed him, he kept him as the apple of his eye. As an eagle stirreth up her nest, fluttereth over her young, spreadeth abroad her wings, taketh them, beareth them on her wings, so the Lord alone did lead him, and there was no strange god with him."

This is a marvelous picture of the wondrous love of God that we cannot stop to go into in detail. Every blessing of life is a love token from God. As the Holy Spirit puts it through the apostle James in James 1:17, "Every good gift and every perfect gift is from above, and cometh down from the Father of lights, with whom is no variableness, neither shadow of turning." When the sun shines with its warmth and light and gladness, lift up your head with joy and say, "This is a token of my Father's love." When you look upon the blossoming flowers, the growing grass, the budding trees in their spring beauty say, "All this beauty with which God adorns the earth, this is another token of God's love to me." When you feel health and strength coursing through your veins, look up and thank God again for this another token of His love. The countless blessings that come to us all every day of our lives, most of them unnoticed in our blindness and ingratitude, are all tokens of His great and constant love.

God's Love Is Manifested in Chastening Us When We Forget Him and Wander from Him and Fall into Sin

In the second place, *God's love to His children—yes, to those also who are not yet His children—is manifested in His chastening us when we forget Him and wander from Him and fall into sin.* This comes out very clearly in that beautiful passage, Hebrews 12:6–10, "For whom the Lord loveth he chasteneth, and scourgeth every son whom he receiveth. If ye endure chastening, God dealeth with you as with sons; for what son is he whom the father chasteneth not? But if ye be without the chastisement, whereof all are partakers, then are ye bastards, and not sons. Furthermore, we have had fathers of our flesh which corrected us, and we gave them reverence: shall we not much rather be in subjection unto the Father of spirits, and live? For they verily for a few days chastened us after their own pleasure; but he for our profit, that we might be partakers of his holiness." Here we see that God's love manifests itself in chastening us, and in sending us trial and pain and bereavement and sorrow. Many cannot see in their many and great afflictions any proof of God's love. It seems to them that God does not love them to allow them to suffer such awful and, sometimes, such appalling griefs and trials, but they who so think are very blind.

Do we not chasten our own beloved children? Do we not do it because we love them and for their good? It would oftentimes be far easier for us not to do it. It would spare our feelings, for we suffer far more than they do when we punish them if we are true parents. Some parents are so unloving and so self-centered that they allow their children to go unpunished in their folly and sin in order to spare their own feelings. But not so our heavenly Father. He really loves us, wisely loves us, and so chastens us for our highest good. And sometimes, when our conduct makes it necessary, He very severely chastises us, or as the Bible puts it, *"scourges"* us. Every wise man thanks God for His chastening love, even in its severest manifestations.

For twelve years or more God spared my wife and myself and our family in our home life from serious sickness. We had gone through epidemics of many kinds unscathed. When threatened with croup, scarlet fever, typhoid fever, diphtheria, and other diseases, we had cried to God, and He had given deliverance again and again. But a day came when God permitted diphtheria to enter our home. A few short hours after the real character of the disease was discovered, He chose to take away from us a beautiful child and to take her away when we thought all danger of death was past. It was a stunning blow, just twenty-four years ago this week. March 17 never comes around without our thinking of it. For the first time the family circle was broken. The body of our child had been carried from our happy home and laid away in the lonely cemetery. Why did God permit it? Because He loved us. We needed it.

The following Sunday night I spoke on Hebrews 12:6: "For whom the Lord loveth he chasteneth, and scourgeth every son whom he receiveth." This chastisement, yes this scourging, led to deep heart searchings and discovery of failure, and thereby led to confession of sin. It led also to new consecration and love for souls and devotion to God. It brought the answer to prayers that had been ascending to Him for years. It was one of the things that led to my leaving Chicago a few years later to enter upon a worldwide ministry. If God had not in His infinite wisdom and love taken our greatly beloved child, our rarely beautiful and gifted child, from us, I think I would never have seen China, Japan, Australia, New Zealand, India, and the marvelous work of God in these countries, and the great work of God that followed in England, Ireland, Wales, Germany and many other places. God's judgments are "unsearchable . . . and his ways past finding out!" (Rom. 11:33). But they are always wise and loving, though we for the time cannot understand how. All of God's seemingly severe dealings with us came from the wise and wondrous love of God, and we both saw it and praised Him. There is no kinder manifestation of the love of God than His chastening us when we forget Him or wander from Him or become immersed in the world.

One beautiful spring day years ago a friend of mine in Ohio asked me to take a drive with him. We drove out into the country to a quiet cemetery. We entered and went to a remote corner of the cemetery and there found side-by-side three graves—one the grave of an adult and the other two of children. They were the graves of that man's wife and his two little girls, all the family he had at the time in the world, with the exception of one little boy. We knelt beside the graves in prayer. As we drove back to town that man said to me, "Brother Torrey, I pity the man whom God has not chastened."

What did he mean? He meant this: He had been a man of the world, an honorable, highly respected man, but a thoroughgoing worldling. Diphtheria came into his home. It took one of his little daughters. As she lay in her casket the father knelt beside it and promised God that he would become a Christian. But when the first bitterness of the sorrow had passed he forgot his vow. Again sickness and death entered his home. This time the second daughter died. Beside her coffin he renewed his vow and kept it. He came to know the joy that every true Christian knows, to have the glorious hope for eternity that only the Christian has. He became, I think, take it all in all, the most active and efficient Christian in the community, and it all came from God's chastening love. He told me again and again that his favorite text of Scripture was, "Whom the Lord loveth he chasteneth." Ah, friends, if some affliction has come upon you see in it a token of God's love and learn the sweet lessons He would teach by this sorrow.

The Love of God Is Manifested by His Sympathizing with Us in All Our Afflictions

In the third place, *God's love is manifested in His sympathizing with us in all our afflictions*. This comes out very clearly in a wonderful verse in the Old Testament, "In all their affliction he was afflicted, and the angel of his presence saved them; in his love and in his pity he redeemed them; and he bore them, and carried them all the days of old" (Isa. 63:9). While God in His wise love to us chastens us—yes, even scourges us—when we forget Him and wander into sin and worldliness, nevertheless He deeply sympathizes with us in every sorrow and trial and heartache that our sin brings upon us. "In all [our] affliction he [is] afflicted." It may be His own hand that sends the affliction, as it was in the passage just read. We need the affliction. It does us good, so He sends it. But He suffers with us in it. *God is the one great sympathizer*, "In all [our] affliction he [is] afflicted."

In our own sorrow, we had many, very many sympathizing human friends and letters and telegrams of heartfelt sympathy poured in upon us. But no one sympathized with us so fully, so tenderly, so deeply, so intelligently as God Himself. He saw what no human eye could see and entered into it all. And there were very many tender little ministries of His in those days of profound sorrow and many wondrous great ministries also. No human being will ever know what Mrs. Torrey and I passed through the night following the burial of our little child and the next morning. The waters were deep. It seemed as if they would go over our heads, but One walked beside us. It was God. He suffered with us. He kept His Word: "When thou passest through the waters, I will be with thee; and through the rivers, they shall not overflow thee; when thou walkest through the fire, thou shalt not be burned, neither shall the flame kindle upon thee" (Isa. 43:2).

Friends, some of you are in deep sorrow, some in sorrow of one kind and some in sorrow of an entirely different kind, but I want to tell you one and all that God sympathizes with you all in your sorrow whatever it may be. It may seem to you that no one sympathizes with you, that no one even understands, that no one cares, and that may be true of men, but it is not true of God. He understands it all and enters into it all. "Our Father cares."

A woman came to see me at the hotel where I was stopping in Bendigo, Australia. She told me that an awful sorrow had come into her life, but that she could not tell it to anyone there, for they all knew her. But I was a stranger and would soon leave the place, and her burden was so heavy she felt that she must have the sympathy of someone, and so she had come to me. It was a terrible story that she told me. She was passing through one of the greatest sorrows that ever overtakes any true woman, and her heart was nearly crushed. When she had finished that sad story she said to me, "I feel better now that there is someone who knows my sorrow and can sympathize with me." I said to her, "I do indeed sympathize with you. I am glad you came and told me the story that I might help you bear your burden. But," I added, "there is One who has known all about it from the beginning. God has known all about it and He has sympathized with you all the time." Oh, it is true, not a sorrow, not a heartache, not a disappointment, not a calamity, not a grief, ever comes to us but our heavenly Father knows it all, knows it in all its details, and sympathizes with us in all the suffering. He Himself suffers far more than we suffer.

God's Love Is Manifested in His Never Forgetting Those Whom He Loves

In the fourth place, *God's love is manifested in His never forgetting those whom He loves.* This He Himself tells us in the wonderful words in Isaiah 49:15–16: "Can a woman forget her sucking child, that she should not have compassion on the son of her womb? Yea, they may forget, yet will I not forget thee. Behold, I have graven thee upon the palms of my hands; thy walls are continually before me." God sometimes seems to forget, but He never does. We cry and no answer comes. The heavens seem to be as brass above our heads, but God has not forgotten. *He never forgets.* A mother may forget her child, though that is not likely; yet she may. But God has said, "Yet will I not forget thee." He has said furthermore, "Behold, I have graven thee upon the palms of my hands."

God's Love Is Manifested in His Forgiving Our Sins

In the fifth place, *God's love is manifested in His forgiving our sins.* Hezekiah cried to the Lord: "Behold, for peace I had great bitterness, but thou hast in love to my soul delivered it from the pit of corruption; for thou hast cast all my sins behind thy back" (Isa. 38:17). God stands ready in His love to pardon the sins of the vilest sinner. There are two things, and only two, which in His love He demands as a condition of that pardon. They are, first, that we forsake our sins; second, that we turn to Him in faith and surrender to His will. Listen to His own word: "Let the wicked forsake his way, and the unrighteous man his thoughts, and let him return unto the LORD, and he will have mercy upon him; and to our God; for he will abundantly pardon" (Isa. 55:7). God will not pardon our sins if we hold on to them. There is a theory regarding God's love current in the world that has no warrant in the Word of God, namely, that because "God is love," He will pardon and save all men, whether they repent and believe on Jesus Christ or not.

This theory is wholly and utterly unscriptural. To believe it you must give up the Bible. But if you give up the Bible you must give up your belief that "God is love," for it is from the Bible, and from the Bible alone, that we learn that "God is love." There is absolutely no other proof that "God is love" than that the Bible says so. That is proof enough, for the Bible can be easily proven to be the Word of God. But if you give up the Bible and are logical, you must give up your belief that "God is love." For when the Bible is gone, the belief that "God is love" has no foundation of any kind. But if you retain the Bible you cannot believe that God will pardon and save all men whether they repent or not.

The most illogical system in the world (except Unitarianism) is Universalism. It starts out with the Bible statement that "God is love" as its foundation stone. Then it goes to work to discredit the Bible by rejecting other plain statements in it—statements about hell and the future state of those who reject Christ. By doing that it undermines the authority of the Bible, and thus undermines the foundation of our faith that "God is love." In other words, it tries to build up a superstructure by undermining its foundation. Give up the Bible and there is no proof that "God is love," and so Universalism goes by the board. Believe in the Bible, and you must believe in hell, and so Universalism goes by the board.

Take either horn of the dilemma you please and Universalism has absolutely no foundation. The very love of God, God's love to the righteous and His love to His Son Jesus Christ demands that if men persist in sin and persist in the rejection of His Son Jesus Christ that they be separated from the righteous and punished. *The love of God makes hell a necessity if men persist in sin.* And, if they persist eternally in sin, it makes *eternal* hell a necessity. And it is psychologically certain, as well as clearly revealed in the Bible, that if men persist in sin beyond a certain point they will persist in sin eternally.

But if the vilest sinner repents, God will pardon. He

says so. He goes so far as to say in Isaiah 1:18: "Come now, and let us reason together, saith the LORD: though your sins be as scarlet, they shall be as white as snow; though they be red like crimson, they shall be as wool." A man once said to me, "My sins are too great for God to pardon." I answered, "I do not wish you to think that your sins are any less than you now think they are—no doubt they are even greater than you think—but I want you to see that great as your sins are, God's pardoning love is greater still."

How often God proved this in the Bible. David's sin was great. It was monstrous. He was an adulterer and a murderer, yet God pardoned him. Manasseh's sin was exceedingly great. He hated God and he hated God's people. He made the streets of Jerusalem to run with the blood of God's servants, yet God pardoned him (2 Kings 24:3–4; cf. 2 Chron. 33:1–13). Saul of Tarsus was a great sinner. He hated Jesus Christ. He persecuted the disciples of Jesus Christ and took part in their murder. He was a bold blasphemer and compelled others to blaspheme, yet God pardoned him. So down through the centuries many of the vilest sinners this world has ever seen have repented, and God has pardoned them. There sit in this building tonight men and women who have gone down into the deepest depths of sin, but God has pardoned and saved them. They sit here tonight rejoicing in His pardoning love, knowing that their every sin is blotted out. Furthermore, they have been transformed by the power of His grace.

God's Love Was Manifested in His Giving His Only Begotten Son to Die for Us

In the sixth place, *God's love was manifested in His giving His only begotten Son to die in our place.* As the Spirit of God puts it in John 3:16: "For God so loved the world, that he gave his only begotten Son, that whosoever believeth in him should not perish, but have everlasting life." And again we read in Romans 8:32: "He that spared not his own Son, but delivered him up for us all." And we read in 1 John 4:10: "Herein is love, not that we loved God, but that he loved us, and sent his Son to be the propitiation for our sins." And away back in the prophetic vision of the Old Testament, seven hundred years before the Savior was born, we read: "All we like sheep have gone astray; we have turned every one to his own way; and Jehovah hath [made to strike] on him the iniquity of us all" (Isa. 53:6). This manifestation of God's love is greatest of all. This manifestation of God's love is stupendous. It seems past believing, but we know it is true. God made the greatest sacrifice in His power for our good. He made the greatest sacrifice in the world's history, He *gave up* that which was dearest to Him, *His own Son.*

No earthly son was ever so dear to his father as Jesus Christ was dear to God. I have a son, an only son, and I love him. But my love for my boy is but the faintest adumbration of God's love to Jesus Christ. And yet God gave that only begotten Son, that eternally beloved Son, up for you and me. Gave Him up to die—to die an awful death, an appalling death. Gave Him up to be crushed by the weight of humanity's sin and guilt. And for what purpose did He give Him up? "That whosoever believeth in him should not perish, but have everlasting life." God has done everything in His power to provide everlasting life for each one of us. If we do not have it, it is our own fault. God has exhausted the resources of infinite wisdom and infinite love and infinite power to provide everlasting life for you and me. You and I can have it for the taking.

Such is the love of God, very inadequately described. But I wish to ask a question in closing. The question is this: *What are you going to do with that wondrous love of God tonight?* Our guilt never looks so black as when seen in the dazzling light of God's amazing love. To be a sinful man or woman seems bad enough, to despise and break God's holy and excellent laws seems bad enough. But the worst thing about men and women out of Christ—the most shocking thing, the most horrible thing—the most damnable and damning thing about men and women out of Christ is, that *they are trampling under foot the love of God.*

What would you think of a man who had a true and loving mother—a mother who had done everything for him, a mother who had made every sacrifice for him, a mother who had impoverished herself and imperiled and wasted her life for him—and then he despised that love, rejected that love, sneered at that love, denied that love, and sought to discredit that love? Would you not say that that man was a wretch? But no mother's love is so great and wonderful as the love of God to you and me. No mother ever made a sacrifice for her child as great as God has made for you and me. Now what will you do with that love tonight? Will you accept it or despise it? Will you put your trust in it or spurn it? Will you open your heart to it or spit upon it? What will you do with it?

Oh, men and women, are you rejecting Christ? Are you trampling under foot the wondrous love of God revealed by giving His Son to die on Calvary's cross for you? If you are, what have you to say for yourselves? Oh, give up your awful treatment of this glorious Son of God, and accept Him now as your personal Savior. Surrender to Him as your Lord and Master. Begin the confession of Him, a confession that most of you should have begun long, long ago. Go out from this place tonight to serve Him all the remainder of your days with all your strength.

Amazing Love!

George Campbell Morgan (1863–1945) was the son of
a British Baptist preacher and preached his first sermon
when he was thirteen years old. He had no formal
training for the ministry, but his tireless devotion to the
study of the Bible helped him to become one of the
leading Bible teachers of his day. Rejected by the
Methodists, he was ordained into the Congregational
ministry. He was associated with Dwight L. Moody in
the Northfield Bible Conferences and as an itinerant
Bible teacher. He is best known as the pastor of the
Westminster Chapel, London (1904–1917 and 1933–
1945). During his second term there, he had D. Martyn
Lloyd-Jones as his associate.

Morgan published more than sixty books and
booklets, and his sermons are found in *The Westminster
Pulpit* (London: Hodder and Stoughton, 1906–1916).
This sermon was taken from volume 1.

George Campbell Morgan

6

AMAZING LOVE!

But God commendeth his love toward us, in that, while
we were yet sinners, Christ died for us (Romans 5:8).

DURING THE PAST WEEK I received one letter which
especially arrested my attention. It was unsigned, and I
want to read it to you. It is very brief, very pointed, and
seems to me to breathe the spirit of restless and
disappointed rebellion. The writer says:

> The writer begs leave to call to the Rev. Campbell
> Morgan's remembrance a statement he made last
> Sunday evening, viz., "My Friend has proved His love
> to me so as to bring conviction to my heart." Then why
> does He not convince every person of His love? Why is
> He not just to all?

The text I have read tonight is my answer to that question, and I was very careful last Sunday night to state
that fact. In speaking of my Friend I said two things concerning His love. First, He has declared His love to my
surprise, and then I made use of these actual words:

> He has demonstrated His love so as to bring conviction
> to my heart. Whether I have responded or not is not
> the question for the moment. I simply state the fact.
> "God commendeth his love toward us, in that, while
> we were yet sinners, Christ died for us."

Thus it will be seen that, when I said that my Friend
had brought conviction of His love to my heart, I made
the statement upon the basis of the text which I take
tonight. I do not regard that the thinking of that letter
is lonely, even though the writing of it is singular. I can

well imagine that many people would go away last Sunday evening saying in their hearts practically the same things. "The preacher declared that God had demonstrated His love to the conviction of his heart, but He has not done so in my experience. If not, why not?" To that attitude of mind I want to say that the proof given to me of the love of God has been given to all. I did not mean to say that in some flaming vision of the night or apocalypse of the day God had done for me what He had not done for others.

I suppose there are people even in this age who do see visions. I have never seen them. I suppose there are even today those who seem to hear, and perhaps do hear, voices which others do not hear. I am not one of such, and I should be very sorry for any man or woman to imagine that I intended to say that I had been privileged by God in any way that they had not. My Friend's proof of His love is given not to me alone, but to all men. No proof in mystic words spoken in loneliness to my own heart, and no proof by some sudden and exceptional vision of glory could begin to be so conclusive to my reason as the great proof that belongs to all quite as much as it belongs to me. I venture to say—I know I speak within the realm of the finite and limited and human, yet I say it of profoundest conviction—God Himself could not have thought of any other way to prove His love so conclusive as the way He has taken.

Will you let me in all love and tenderness, and yet with great earnestness, say to you, my friend who wrote to me—and to all such—that if God's love has not carried conviction to your heart, I think it is because you have not taken time to consider that great proof. You have heard of it, you have sung of it. You could recite the proof texts, my text and the text in John, and many other such. "God so loved the world, that he gave his only begotten Son" (John 3:16a). That is the proof. "God commendeth his love toward us, in that, while we were yet sinners, Christ died for us." That is the proof. I have no other. Hear me, that is not idly spoken. I have no other.

I do not find the proof of God's personal love to me in

nature. There are proofs in nature when once I have found His heart of grace. Then every flower seems to me to sing of His love, and all the rhythmic order of the universe becomes one great anthem of His tenderness. I never heard the song of the flowers or the anthem of the universe until this proof had brought me low and convinced me of His love. I have no proof but this. Yet I say to you again, speaking experimentally, my Friend has proved His love to the satisfaction of my heart in such full and perfect measure that I have no alternative, so help me God, other than that of yielding myself to Him—spirit, soul, and body, lover to lover in an embrace that makes us one forever.

I cannot help thinking, if you will let me repeat it, that if this proof has not carried conviction, it is because you have not taken time to think of it and consider it. You may believe it theoretically. You may never have quarreled with the simple statement, with the perpetual, almost monotonous, message of the evangel. But have you ever considered the proof of God's love? To ask such a question as this, to make such a suggestion as this, is, of course, at least to carry to your minds the thought that I am going to try to lead you in the way of consideration. So I am, and yet I feel I never had a harder task or a more impossible.

What can be said when the Scripture has spoken? There is nothing to add to the text. There is great danger of detracting from its infinite music by any attempt to analyze it and break it up. O that we may hear it sung into our deepest heart tonight by that infinite spirit of music, the Spirit of God. "God commendeth"—recommends, demonstrates, proves—"his love toward us, in that, while we were yet sinners, Christ died for us." I cannot add to that. There is nothing more to be said. It is the speech of infinite and eternal love. When I read it I am inclined to bow my head and say, "The LORD is in his holy temple; let all the earth keep silence before him" (Hab. 2:20). Yet I must deliver my message, tremblingly and falteringly, and honestly wishing I need not say any more.

Notice, first, the persons involved in the declaration—God and the sinner. The spaciousness of the text is its difficulty. The infinite distances appall us when we begin to attempt to traverse them. We sometimes speak as though the supreme thought of distance were expressed in the words, "at the poles asunder." The poles asunder! That is but a handbreadth, but a span! God and the sinner. That is the supreme distance.

Notice, in the next place, the fact declared. Four words declare it. Four words that any little child who has been to school for one year could spell out—four words in our language all so tiny that a child can lisp them. Yet heaven is richer for their utterance, and all the thunder of the music of the seraphim is as nothing to that contained in them. All the mystery of human pain through piled up centuries is only palest gray by the side of the deep, dense darkness of this announcement, "Christ died for us." Finally, notice the truth declared in the text: "God commendeth his love toward us." I cannot, I do not, believe that if you will quietly try this evening to traverse that threefold line of consideration you can write to me again and say, "God has not demonstrated His love to me."

Notice first the persons involved. How shall I speak reverently and yet with boldness of God? It seems to me that the great apostle of love, John, the mystic, the seer, the man of vision, has given us in the briefest sentences the sublimest truths concerning God. I am not going to attempt to deal with these sentences, yet I want to quote them. John tells us the story of the essence of deity in this brief word, "God is love" (1 John 4:8, 16). That is the subject in question tonight. John tells us the nature of God as well as His essence in words equally short and simple, "God is life" (see John 1:4; 1 John 1:2). And once again John tells us the character of God in another sentence as simple, "God is light" (1 John 1:5). How dare I drape such declarations with the verbiage of explanation? It seems to me as though the Spirit through the chosen apostle of love took up the simplest words of human speech and lifted them above all rhetoric and eloquence and explanation and exposition, and focused in them all the light and splendor and glory concerning God, of whom it is possible for man to stand in the presence and live.

God is life, essential life. In the Word is included all the facts of power that we try to express in other ways: all the facts of wisdom that so often appall us when we have tracked its footsteps through immensity, and that overwhelming fact of His sovereignty that we are so slow to learn and acknowledge. God is life. Not that He has it, or has been it, or even lives it, but He is life. This I am not considering now, for it does not seem to me that we shall catch the marvel of my text if we simply consider the fact of the life of God as it is manifest in all power and wisdom and supremacy. To be told that a Being of infinite power loves is not astonishing, even though His love be set upon a finite thing. To be told that a Being of infinite intelligence loves does not appall me, even though His love be set upon some foolish creature of His own hand. To be told that a sovereign, supreme Being loves is not amazing, even though His love be set upon those who are subject to His throne. Therefore I pass from the sentence that speaks of the essence, "God is love," and the sentence that speaks of the nature, "God is life," to the final sentence which speaks of character, "God is light." The moment I have uttered it or read it, the moment the thought it suggests passed before me, I begin to be astonished at the declaration that He loves me.

"God is light, and in him is no darkness at all." How shall I speak of that light and what it really means? It is best of all to catch the words of Holy Scripture and let them suggest, at least to my heart, something of the infinite and awful purity of God. He is holy and righteous. He is true and faithful. Holy—right in character. Righteous—right in conduct. True—the essential fact concerning Himself. Faithful—His loyalty in all His dealings with created things to the uttermost bound of His universe, to that essential fact of truth in His own being. The God of the universe—infinite in power, infinite in wisdom—is, above all else, infinite in holiness. If the statement of the truth does not appall us, it is because our sensibility to holiness is blunted by our own sin. If these words can easily pass our lips and we never tremble, the lack of trembling is evidence of paralysis in all the higher sensibilities of the spiritual nature. If only we knew what holiness meant? If we could understand what righteousness essentially means? If only we understood the real meaning of "truth in the inward parts" (Ps. 51:6), of faithfulness in the least detail of the activity of power, we would be appalled by the thought of the essential holiness of God. *God, infinite in holiness.* Let the broken and incomplete sentence suffice.

Then I pass to the end of my text and find this word "sinners." What are sinners? Those who in character are the exact opposite of God, though they are kin to Him by nature. Here is the marvel. By nature man is kin of God. Do not be afraid of the great word that the apostle quoted on Mars Hill. By first creation man is "offspring of God," kin to God, related to God. As in His nature there is essential power, in my life there is power. As in His nature there is wisdom, in my life there are knowledge and wisdom. As in His nature there are supremacy and government, so in every human being there is the capacity for government. For man is the crown of creation, the king of the cosmos, made for cooperation with God in government and dominion over all the far-reaching life that stretches—lost territory—beneath his feet.

Such is man in his nature. But what of his character? Though he is kin to God in nature, all his character is unlike God. Unholy instead of holy. Unrighteous instead of righteous. Untrue instead of true. Unfaithful instead of faithful. Contrary to God in choices and conduct. I am not going to discuss the theory of the "how," I am simply stating the fact of human life. Even though in these days some of us may be inclined to quarrel with the phraseology of sacred Scripture and the terminology of the older school of theology, the fact remains, men "go astray as soon as they be born, speaking lies" (Ps. 58:3).

There is no man here who will test his past character

and conduct—I will not say by the white light of God's existence, but by his own ideal of truth and uprightness and purity—and dare stand erect and say, "I have never sinned." There is no man in this house who dare say that, whatever his religion, or lack of religion. Men everywhere are ready to admit the fact of sin. We have been told quite recently that in these days men do not want to hear about sin. Men are putting sin out of their vocabulary as a word and are attempting to put it out of their thinking as a fact. But they cannot put it out of your experience. Drop it out of your vocabulary if you will be so foolish. Cease taking account of it in your arrangements if you will be so mad. It will be the madness of the ostrich that hides its head in the sand of the desert and dreams it is unseen because it cannot see.

Now mark what this means as to contrast. By the highest standards of human experience the sinner ought to be objectionable and loathsome to God. Purity—and we are down on the low level of human thinking—does and ought to hate impurity. The man of high ideals must hold in supreme contempt the man of base and ignoble ideals. To me it is first of all inconceivable that infinite purity can care for me because I am impure. Apart from the cross of Christ you will never persuade me that God loves me. I am not blaming God for not loving me. I would not suggest that He ought to love me. I would not lend my lips to the blasphemy of saying that He ought to love me because He made me. He made me kin to Himself with environment in His own being and the inheritance of His own might, stronger than any other environment and inheritance I have entered into. Still, I am impure. I have been selfish and sinful, and am undone in the fiber of my moral being.

It is inconceivable to me that the pure can love the impure. I cannot, save as His love enters into my life and enables me. The measure of my purity—it is faint, God knows—but the measure of it is the measure in which impurity is hateful. Here are the supreme mystery and the supreme miracle, not only of the evangel as it is declared, but of the experience of all such as share its mystery and become themselves like God in that they, too, love those who are unlike Him and unlike themselves. Mark the persons involved: God, infinite in holiness and purity and uprightness, and sinners such as are kin to Him in nature and utterly unlike Him and opposed to Him in character.

Now come to the fact declared in this text, the central fact of all your Bible. The fact, the first dreams of which you find in Eden, and the last glory of which flames in the Apocalypse. "Christ died for us." "Christ died." How am I going to speak of that? Do not be angry when I say that some of you are almost weary of hearing this. You are almost inclined to say, "Is this all? We know all this." We do not begin to know it. There is nothing else to say when this is said. Therefore, God help us to be careful how we say it, and how we hear it. The matter of first importance is that we are very careful what we mean when we say "Christ." It is of equal importance that we are very careful what we mean when we say, "died." If I take this simplest phrase in holy Scripture, "Christ died," and utter the word "Christ," I think simply of a peasant of Galilee. When I utter the word "died," I think of such a death as I have seen when my own loved ones passed. But I have not heard the music, have not seen the wonder, have not begun to understand how God commends His love.

With great solemnity, and speaking under deep conviction, I warn you never to forget that when you speak of Jesus you also speak of God. God was in Christ, not as He is in me even by His grace, but in that fuller and infinite sense which the apostle expresses in the grandeur of that word in the Colossian epistle. "It was the good pleasure of the Father that in Him should all the fulness dwell corporeally." Oh, I cannot understand it. No philosophy man ever invented can contain it. If you rob the word "Christ" of that significance, your Gospel will fall to pieces. Remember that this is God in Christ. The Man of Nazareth, very man, perfect man, man as I am man, was God's revelation to me of Himself. The Son of God was incarnate in the Man of Nazareth, and the Son of God is today still related to that self-same Man of Nazareth in the place where men gather in the home of God.

But you have something larger here than the mere Man of Nazareth, you have Christ. The name is the mystic symbol of Godhead bent in humility to redemption's work. Christ, the Son of God who is of the essence of God, who was with God in the measureless deeps and infinitudes of bygone eternity, who was God, and who, in a mystery profounder than the mystery of the rolling ages, became flesh and dwelt among men. "Christ"—do not put any small human measurement upon this word, or you will rob the evangel of its music. You may well sit down and tell me that God has not proved His love to you if you think little of Christ. It is little thinking of Christ that has degraded our conception of the meaning of His death. "Christ died," and if you stand in front of the Roman gibbet and watch the ebbing of the life of the man until presently you say, "He is dead," and if you imagine that is all that is meant, your eyes are very blind. You have seen very little. He Himself said that the physical is not death. He did not ever speak of such as death, but always as falling asleep. In His thinking and teaching, and in the apostolic thinking and teaching that immediately succeeded it, death was something profounder than physical dissolution.

What is death? Death is that in which a man may be, while yet alive in the physical realm. A man can be dead in trespasses and sins. Death is that condition in which a woman may be while in the height of the London season. "She that liveth in pleasure is dead while she liveth" (1 Tim. 5:6). Death is not dissolution of the body. It is severance of the spirit from God, the sense of homelessness, the sense of friendlessness, the one all-inclusive agony of loss, of lack, and of failure. Christ—and do not forget the meaning of the word—died. Listen, "My God, my God, why hast thou forsaken me?" (Matt. 27:46; Mark 15:34). The sense of homelessness, loss, the infinite agony of loneliness.

But you say to me, "You told us a moment ago that this was God." Yes, I repeat it. Then you say, "What can

He mean when He says, 'My God, my God, why hast thou forsaken me?' How can God say that to God?" Here are the mystery and the marvel of the unveiling of infinite love as you will find it nowhere else. I pray you do not imagine that this Person on the cross is other than God. After hearing that human speech in which the Infinite and Eternal sobs itself out in the little language of a fallen race, what do I find? I find that God has lost Himself to find man. I find that God has gathered into His own consciousness the whole unutterable issue of sin. Christ died. He did not cease to be. God in Christ, who had blessed men with a touch and had wooed men with winsomeness, now dies as He finds the place of loneliness, of homelessness, of infinite lack. Yes, verily the old prophetic word is fulfilled there in the sight of heaven and earth and hell in the experience of God, "The pains of hell got hold upon me" (Ps. 116:3). "Christ died." And yet you say that God has not proved His love to you.

Now mark the infinite reaches of this Gospel—God and the sinner. We see the infinite gulf, and we state, according to the very highest and best conception we have of things, that God ought to count the sinner loathsome. What is the truth? When there was no eye to pity, His eye pitied. When there was no arm to save, His arm brought salvation. What is the truth? Hear it, man, woman, doubting of God's love. The God of infinite purity bent in the mystery of incarnation, and in the cross, to the condition of the impure. He gathered into His own experience and consciousness all the immeasurable and unutterable issues of sin. "God commendeth his love toward us, in that, while we were yet sinners, Christ died for us." Oh, for such love let rocks and hills their lasting silence break!

"God commendeth his love." Can you explain to me in any other way than by the answer that love was the inspiration, the mystery of that descent and that great death? I say to you tonight that to me there is no other explanation of that death. "Scarcely for a righteous man will one die: yet peradventure for a good man some would even dare to die" (Rom. 5:7). Such is the prologue of my text, and mark the emphasis, "But God commendeth his love toward us, in that, while we were yet sinners, Christ died for us." "His love"—there is no other like it. Here is the quality found nowhere else—"His love." You cannot commend anyone else's love in this way. I ask you again, does that truth prove anything other than love? You tell me that that truth is proof of God's righteousness. I tell you, "No." You tell me truth is proof of God's wisdom. I say, "No, not supremely." You tell me that truth is proof of God's power. "Not finally." Yet God's righteousness is vindicated in it, wisdom is manifested, power is operative. You tell me that the Atonement was necessary because of righteousness. And I say, "No, God's righteousness might have been vindicated by the annihilation of evil. All the infinite righteousness of God might have been perfectly satisfied if He had swept out the things that insulted His righteousness." But listen, "How can I let thee go?" That is the language, not of righteousness, but of love. "He commendeth his love." The apostle understood the deep truth. Though this is the great apostle of righteousness he does not say, "He commendeth His righteousness," but "He commendeth his love toward us." I stand in the presence of my text, and in the presence of that eternal wonder, and I say my Friend has demonstrated His love to the satisfaction of my heart. I know now that He loves me.

Surprised? Oh, my God, how growingly surprised I am. Amazing love! Why did He love me? I really do not know. But He did, and He does. Why should He care for me? I have been so selfish, so impure in my thinking and desire. Why, I cannot tell. But this I know, He loves me. You may persuade me on many things, and you may dissuade me from some convictions, but I challenge you to dissuade me here. My Friend loves me. I am in His heart as well as in His power. I am in His love as well as in His light. You ask me how I know it. I take you, not to the infinite spaces where stars march in rhythmic order, not to the hedgerow where God smiles in flowers, but to the rough and brutal cross of Calvary, to the hour of the dying of the Christ. "God commendeth his love toward us, in that, while we were yet sinners, Christ died for us." My friends, such love is royal, and royal love makes claims upon loyalty. What shall I do in answer to that love? We have often sung together:

> Were the whole realm of nature mine,
>   That were a present far too small;
> Love so amazing, so divine,
>   Demands my soul, my life, my all!

Have we not sung that wrong in two ways? Have we not sung it first as though we would say, "I cannot give Him so great a thing as the realm of nature; I can give only myself to Him?" That is wrong. He counts you, bruised and broken, sinful, dying man, more than the whole realm of nature. When one day He held the infinite balances in His hand, He said, "What shall it profit a man, if he shall gain the whole world, and lose his own soul?" (Mark 8:36). That is His estimate. God so loves you that He would not feel Himself enriched if He could save the whole realm of nature and lose you. How do I know that? Because He gave something infinitely more than the whole realm of nature, He gave Himself in His Son for you. If you want to know your value by the measurements of love, God measured you by Himself. When next you sing that verse, do not sing it as though you had nothing to give—if you have yourself to give. If you have yourself to give, give yourself.

That is all He wants. Have we not sung that verse wrongly in the next place by singing, "Love so amazing, so divine, demands my soul, my life, my all," without the answering abandonment? My brother, my sister, answer that love tonight, not only by singing of its demands, but by giving all you are to it. Give yourself, with all your wounds and bruises, with all your weakness and frailty. Answer that love, and that love will remake you until at last you shall be meet for the dwelling of the saints in light. May God in His infinite grace speak this word to us as no human voice can speak it.

NOTES

Unknowable Love Known to Love

Alexander Maclaren (1826–1910) was one of Great Britain's most famous preachers. While pastoring the Union Chapel, Manchester (1858–1903), he became known as "the prince of expository preachers." Rarely active in denominational or civic affairs, Maclaren invested his time in studying the Word in the original languages and sharing its truths with others in sermons that are still models of effective expository preaching. He published a number of books of sermons and climaxed his ministry by publishing his monumental *Expositions of Holy Scripture*.

This message was taken from *Christ in the Heart,* published by Funk and Wagnalls Company in 1902.

Alexander Maclaren

7

UNKNOWABLE LOVE
KNOWN TO LOVE

That ye . . . may be able to comprehend with all saints
what is the breadth, and length, and depth, and height;
and to know the love of Christ, which passeth knowledge
(Ephesians 3:17–19a).

THIS CONSTITUTES THE THIRD of the petitions in this great
prayer of Paul's. Each rises above and is a consequence
of the preceding and leads on to and is a cause or occasion
of the subsequent one.

The two former petitions for inward strength have been
communicated by a divine Spirit in order that Christ may
dwell in our hearts, and so we may be rooted and grounded
in love. The result of these desires being realized in our
hearts is here set forth in two clauses which are substan-
tially equivalent in meaning. "To comprehend" may be
taken as meaning nearly the same as "to know," only that
perhaps the former expresses an act more purely intellectual. And "the breadth, and length, and depth, and height"
are the unmeasurable dimensions of the love which in the
second clause is described as "passing knowledge." I purpose to deal with these measures in a separate discourse,
and therefore, I am omitting them from consideration now.

We have, then, mainly two thoughts here: the one, that
only the loving heart in which Christ dwells can know
the love of Christ; the other, that even that heart *cannot* know the love of Christ. The paradox is intentional,
but it is intelligible. Let me deal then, as well as I can,
with these two great thoughts.

Only the Loving Heart Can Know Christ's Love

Now the Bible uses the word *know* to express two
different things. One is what we call mere intellectual

93

perception, or to put it into plainer words, mere head knowledge such as a man may have about any subject of study. The other is a deep and living experience that is possession before it is knowledge, and knowledge because it is possession.

Now the former of these two—the knowledge that is merely the work of the understanding—is, of course, independent of love. A man may know all about Christ and His love without one spark of love in his heart. And there are thousands of people who, as far as the mere intellectual understanding is concerned, know as much about Jesus Christ and His love as the saint who is closest to the Throne, and yet have not one trace of love to Christ in them. That is the kind of people that a widely diffused Christianity and a habit of hearing sermons produce. There are plenty of them here in this chapel this morning who, as far as their heads are concerned, know quite as much of Jesus Christ and His love as any of us do. They could talk about it and argue about it and draw inferences from it. They have gotten the whole system of evangelical Christianity at their fingers' ends. Aye! It is at their fingers' *ends*. It never gets any nearer to them than that.

There is a knowledge with which love has nothing to do, and it is a knowledge that for many people is quite sufficient. "Knowledge puffeth up" (1 Cor. 8:1b), says the apostle. It puffs up into an unwholesome bubble of self-complacency that will one day be pricked and disappear, but "love buildeth up"—a steadfast, slowly-rising, solid fabric. There be two kinds of knowledge: the mere rattle of notions in a man's brain like the seeds of a withered poppy head—very many, very dry, very hard—that will make a noise when you shake it. And there is another kind of knowledge that goes deep down into the heart and is the only knowledge worth calling by the name, and that knowledge is the child, as my text has it, of love.

Now let us think about that for a moment. Love, says Paul, is the parent of all knowledge. Well, now, can we find any illustrations from similar facts in other regions? Yes! I think so. How do we know, really know, any emotions of any sort whatever? Only by experience. You may talk forever about feelings, but you teach nothing about them to those who have not experienced them. The poets of the world have been singing about love ever since the world began. But no heart has learned what love is from even the sweetest and deepest songs. Who that is not a father can be taught paternal love by words, or can come to a perception of it by an effort of mind? And so with all other emotions. Only the lips that have drunk the cup of sweetness or of bitterness can tell how sweet or how bitter it is. Even when they, made wise by experience, speak out their deepest hearts, the listeners are but little the wiser unless they too have been initiated in the same school. Experience is our only teacher in matters of feelings and emotions, as in the lower regions of taste and appetite. A man must be hungry to know what hunger is. He must taste honey or wormwood in order to know the taste of honey or wormwood. In like manner he cannot know sorrow but by feeling its ache, and must love if he would know love. Experience is our only teacher, and her school fees are heavy.

Just as a blind man can never be made to understand the glories of a sunrise, or the light upon the far-off mountains; just as a deaf man may read books about acoustics, but they will not give him a notion of what it is to hear Beethoven, so we must have love *to* Christ before we know what love to Christ is. We must consciously experience the love *of* Christ before we know what the love of Christ is. We must have love *to* Christ in order to have a deep and living possession of the love *of* Christ, though reciprocally it is also true that we must have the love of Christ known and felt by our answering hearts if we are ever to love Him back again.

So in all the play and counterplay of love between Christ and us, and in all the reaction of knowledge and love, this remains true: that we must be rooted and grounded in love before we can know love. We must have Christ dwelling in our hearts in order to have that deep and living possession which, when it is conscious of itself, is knowledge and is forever alien to the loveless heart.

> He must be loved, ere that to you
> He will seem worthy of your love.

If you want to know the blessedness of the love of Christ, love Him and open your hearts for the entrance of His love to you. Love is the parent of the deep, true knowledge.

Of course, before we can love an unseen person and believe in his love, we must know about him by the ordinary means by which we learn about all persons outside the circle of our sight. So before the love that is thus the parent of deep, true knowledge, there must be the knowledge by study and credence of the record concerning Christ, which supplies the facts on which alone love can be nourished. The understanding has its part to play in leading the heart to love, and then the heart becomes the true teacher. He that loves knows God, for God is love. He that is rooted and grounded in love because Christ dwells in his heart will be strengthened to know the love in which he is rooted. The Christ within us will know the love of Christ. We must first "taste," and then we shall "see" that the Lord is good, as the psalmist puts it with deep truth (Ps. 34:8). First, the appropriation and feeding upon God, then the clear perception by the mind of the sweetness in the taste. First the enjoyment, then the reflection on the enjoyment. First the love, and then the consciousness of the love of Christ possessed and the love to Christ experienced. The heart must be grounded in love that the man may know the love that passes knowledge.

Then notice that there is also here another condition for this deep and blessed knowledge laid down in these words, "That ye . . . may be able to comprehend *with all saints.*" That is to say, our knowledge of the love of Jesus Christ depends largely on our sanctity. If we are pure, we shall know. If we are wholly devoted to Him, we should wholly know His love to us. In the measure in which we are pure and holy, we shall know it. This heart of ours is like a reflecting telescope, the least breath upon the mirror will cause all the starry sublimities that it should shadow forth to fade and become dim. The slightest moisture in the atmosphere, though it be quite imperceptible where we stand, will be dense enough to shut out the fair, shining, snowy summits that girdle the horizon and to leave nothing visible but the lowliness and commonplaceness of the prosaic plain.

If you want to know the love of Christ, first of all, that love must purify your souls. But then you must keep your souls pure, assured of this, that only the single eye is full of light. They who are not "saints" grope in the dark even at midday, and while drenched by the sunshine of His love, are unconscious of it altogether. And so we get that miserable and mysterious tragedy of men and women walking through life, as many of you are doing, in the very blaze and focus of Christ's love, and never beholding it nor knowing anything about it.

Observe again the beginning of this path of knowledge, which we have thus traced. There must be, says my text, an indwelling Christ, and so an experience deep and stable of His love. Then we shall know the love that we thus experience. But how does that indwelling come? That is the question for us. The knowledge of His love is blessedness, is peace, is love, is everything, as we shall see in considering the last stage of this prayer. That knowledge arises from our fellowship with and our possession of the love of God, which is in Jesus Christ. How does that fellowship with, and possession of the love of God in Jesus Christ, come? That is the all-important question. What is the beginning of everything? "That Christ may dwell in your hearts by faith" (Eph. 3:17). There is the gate through which you and I may come, and by which we must come if we are to come at all into the possession and perception of Christ's great love.

Here is the path of knowledge. First of all there must be the simple historical knowledge of the facts of Christ's life and death for us, with the Scripture teaching of their meaning and power. And then we must turn these truths from mere notion into life. It is not enough to know the love that God has to us in that lower sense of the word "knowledge." Many of you know that, who never got any blessing out of it all your days, and never will, unless you change. Besides the "knowing" there must be the "believing" of the love. You must translate the notion into a living fact in your experience. You must pass from the simple work of understanding the Gospel to the higher act of faith. You must not be contented with knowing; you must trust. And if you have done that, all the rest will follow. The little, narrow, low doorway of humble self-distrusting faith, through which a man creeps on his knees leaving outside all his sin and his burden, opens out into the temple palace—the large place in which Christ's love is imparted to the soul.

Friends, this doctrine of my text ought to be for every one of us a joy and a gospel. There is no royal road into the sweetness and the depth of Christ's love, for the wise or the prudent. The understanding is no more the organ for apprehending the love of Christ than is the ear the organ for perceiving light, or the heart the organ for learning mathematics. Blessed be God! The highest gifts are not bestowed upon the clever people—on the men of genius and the gifted ones, the cultivated and the re-fined—but they are open for all men. When we say that love is the parent of knowledge and that the condition of knowing the depths of Christ's heart is simple love which is the child of faith, we are only saying, in other words, what the Master embodied in His thanksgiving prayer, "I thank thee, O Father, Lord of heaven and earth, be-cause thou hast hid these things from the wise and pru-dent, and hast revealed them unto babes" (Matt. 11:25).

And that is so, not because Christianity, being a fool-ish system, can only address itself to fools; not because Christianity, contradicting wisdom, cannot expect to be received by the wise and the cultured. But it is so be-cause a man's brains have as little to do with his trust-ful acceptance of the Gospel of Jesus Christ as a man's eyes have to do with his capacity of hearing a voice.

Therefore, seeing that the wise and prudent, and the cultured, and the clever, and the men of genius are always the minority of the race, let us vulgar folk that are neither wise, nor clever, nor cultured, nor geniuses, be thankful that all that has nothing to do with our power of knowing and possessing the best wisdom and the highest treasures. But upon this path the wayfaring man, though a fool, shall not err. All limited understandings and poor, simple, uneducated people, as well as philosophers and geniuses, have to learn love by their hearts and not by their heads. By a sense of need and a humble trust and a daily experience, they have to appropriate and suck out the blessing that lies in the love of Jesus Christ. Blessed be His name! The end of all aristocracies of culture and superciliousness of intellect lies in that great truth that we possess the deepest knowledge and highest wisdom when we love.

Not Even the Loving Heart Can Know the Love of Christ

It "passeth knowledge," says my text. Now I do not suppose that the paradox here of knowing the love of Christ "which passeth knowledge" is to be explained by taking "know" and "knowledge" in the two different senses to which I have already referred, so as that we may experience, and know by conscious experience, that love which the mere understanding is incapable of grasping. That, of course, is an explanation that might be defended, but I take it that it is much truer to the apostle's meaning to suppose that he uses the words "know" and "knowledge" both times in the same sense. And so we get familiar thoughts, which I touch upon very briefly.

Our knowledge of Christ's love, though real, is incomplete, and must always be so. You and I believe, I hope, that Christ's love is not a man's love or, at least, that it is more than a man's love. We believe that it is the flowing out to us of the love of God. We believe that all the fullness of the divine heart pours itself through that narrow channel of the human nature of our Lord and, therefore, that the flow is endless and the Fountain infinite.

I suppose I do not need to show you that it is possible for people to have—and that in fact we do possess—a real, a valid, a reliable knowledge of that which is infinite, although we possess, as a matter of course, no adequate and complete knowledge of it. But I only remind you that we have before us in Christ's love something which, though the understanding is not by itself able to grasp it, yet the understanding led by the heart can lay hold of and can find in it infinite treasures. We can lay our poor hands on His love as a child might lay its tiny palm upon the base of some great cliff, and hold that love in a real grasp of a real knowledge and certitude. But we cannot put our hands around it and feel that we *comprehend* as well as *apprehend*. Let us be thankful that we cannot.

His love can only become to us a subject of knowledge as it reveals itself in its manifestations. Yet after even these manifestations, it remains unuttered and unutterable even by the cross and grave, even by the glory and the throne. "It is as high as heaven; what canst thou do? Deeper than hell; what canst thou know? The measure of it is longer than the earth, and broader than the sea" (Job 11:8–9).

We have no measure by which we can translate into the terms of our experience, and so bring within the grasp of our minds, what was the depth of the step that Christ took at the impulse of His love, from the throne to the cross. We know not what He underwent. We know not, nor ever shall know, what depths of darkness and soul-agony He passed through at the bidding of His all-enduring love to us. Nor do we know the consequences of that great work of emptying Himself of His glory. We have no means by which we can estimate the darkness and the depth of the misery from which we have been delivered, nor the height and the radiance of the glory to which we are to be lifted. And until we can tell and measure by our compasses both of these two extremes of possible human fate, until we have gone down into the deepest abyss of a bottomless pit of growing alienation and misery, and up above the highest reach of all unending progress into light and glory and Godlikeness, we have not stretched our compasses wide enough to touch the two poles of this great sphere, the infinite love of Jesus Christ. So we bow before it. We know that we possess it with a knowledge more sure and certain, more deep and valid, than our knowledge of anything but ourselves. But yet it is beyond our grasp, and towers above us inaccessible in the altitude of its glory, and deep beneath us in the profundity of its condescension.

And, in like manner, we may say that this known love passes knowledge, inasmuch as our experience of it can never exhaust it. We are like the settlers on some great island continent—as, for instance, on the Australian continent for many years after its first discovery—a thin fringe of population around the seaboard here and there, and all the bosom of the land untraversed and unknown. So after all experiences of and all blessed participation in the love of Jesus Christ that come to each of us by our faith, we have but skimmed the surface, but touched the edges. We have received a drop of what, if it should come upon us in fullness of flood like a Niagara of love, would overwhelm our spirits.

So we have within our reach not only the treasure of creatural affections that bring gladness into life when they come, and darkness over it when they depart; we have not only human love that is always lifting its finger to its lips in the act of bidding us adieu. We may possess a love that will abide with us forever. Men die, Christ lives. We can exhaust men; we cannot exhaust Christ. We can follow other objects of pursuit—all of which have limitation to their power of satisfying and pall upon the jaded sense sooner or later, or sooner or later wrenched away from the aching heart. But here is a love into which we can penetrate very deep and fear no exhaustion. It is a sea into which we can jump without dread that, like some rash diver flinging himself into shallow water where he thought there was depth, we may be bruised and wounded. We may find in Christ the endless love that an immortal heart requires. Enter by the low door of faith. Your finite heart will have the joy of an infinite love for its possession, and your mortal life will rise transfigured into an immortal and growing participation in the immortal love of the indwelling and inexhaustible Christ.

NOTES

The Great Enfranchisement

John Henry Jowett (1864–1923) was known during his ministry by some as "the greatest preacher in the English-speaking world." He was born in Yorkshire, England. He was ordained into the Congregational ministry, and his second pastorate was at the famous Carr's Lane Church, Birmingham, where he followed the eminent Dr. Robert W. Dale. From 1911 to 1918, he pastored the Fifth Avenue Presbyterian Church, New York City; from 1918 to 1923, he ministered at Westminster Chapel, London, succeeding G. Campbell Morgan. He wrote many books of devotional messages and sermons.

This message was taken from *Apostolic Optimism,* published by Richard R. Smith, Inc., New York, in 1930.

John Henry Jowett

8

THE GREAT ENFRANCHISEMENT

> Unto him that loveth us, and loosed us from our sins by
> his blood; and he made us to be a kingdom, to be priests
> unto his God and Father; to him be the glory and the
> dominion for ever and ever. Amen (Revelation 1:5b–6
> ASV).

"UNTO HIM THAT LOVETH US." That is where our hopes are
born. That is the background in which we find the base
and the warrant for all our confidence and faith. God
loves us. All effective reasoning concerning human
redemption must begin here. God loves! The beginning
is not to be found in us, in our inclinations and gropings
and resolvings and prayers. These are essential but
secondary. The primary element is the inclination of God.
The fire that warms the hearthstone is not original. It is
derivative and refers us back to the sun. The candle with
which we search for the lost piece of silver is not original
and originating. It is borrowed flame from the great altar
fires of the sun. Earth's broken lights—a candle here, a
lamp there, a fire yonder—all index backward and point
us to the great originating center of solar light and heat.
The lamps and candles and fires that burn in human life,
everything that is bright and genial and aspiring, have
reference backward to some creative and beneficent
source.

"We love him, because he first loved us" (1 John 4:19).
"He first loved!" That is the primary quantity, and every kindly feeling that warms the heart, every pure hope
that illumines the mind, were begotten of that most gracious source. "He first loved!" When did He begin to love
"I have loved thee with an everlasting love" (Jer. 31:3).
Up from the everlasting! "Before I formed thee in the
belly, I knew thee" (1:5). The primordial germ is not a

material plasma or a fire-tuft. Let us trace our pedigree far enough back into the love-purpose of the Everlasting. This is the biblical account of our origin, of the primary movement that gave our being its birth: "He first loved." Nobody comes into the world God-hated. It is possible to come into the world man-hated, or with most reluctant and indifferent welcome. But behind everybody is God, and God is love. Everybody's pedigree begins in love. A glance into origins is a look into love. That is the all-sufficient warrant of human hope and confidence.

"Unto him that loveth us." "Loveth!" Then the gracious sentiment did not exhaust itself with our origin. "Unto him that loveth." The affection is continuous, not spasmodic, but unbroken. There is no abatement of its volume. "The river of God . . . is full of water" (Ps. 65:9), and it flows near the life that it first created. There is a highroad that I knew full well away in the distant north, and a gladsome, shining river keeps it company. Their tracks remain in closest fellowship. They turn and wind together, and at any moment you may step from the dusty highway and drink deep draughts from the limpid stream.

"There is a river, the streams whereof shall make glad the city of God" (Ps. 46:4a). Here is the hard, dusty highway of the individual life, and near it there flows the gladdening river of the Eternal Love. It turns with our turnings, and winds through all the perplexing labyrinths of our intensely varied day. We may ignore the river. We cannot ignore it away. Thrice blessed are they who heed and use it. "They drank of that spiritual Rock that followed them: and that Rock was Christ" (1 Cor. 10:4b). The inspiring resources are always just at hand. The river of love runs just by the hard road. It never parts company with the highway.

"He first loved." "Unto him that loveth." "Having loved . . . he loved them unto the end" (John 13:1b). "I have loved thee with an everlasting love." That is the point to fix the vision when we wish to re-enkindle hope in our ultimate and perfected redemption. "Unto him that loveth us." Love is not an idle sentiment, a sweet languor, a brightly-tinted bubble, sailing in the quiet summer air. Love is energy, throbbing with benevolent purpose and seeking for ever increasing ministries through which to express itself in beneficent service. Love is no effeminate reverie. It is a hungry spirit of sacrifice.

"God so loved . . . that he *gave!*" (John 3:16). That is it. Love is an impartation, a giving sacrifice unconscious of itself. The word "sacrifice" is not to be found in love's vocabulary. Love gives and gives, and takes it as a gracious favor if you will receive the gift. Love never sits down to contemplate its sacrifices. It only sits down to think out new fields of service. Love is tremendous energy hungrily keen for the detection of need that it might fill the gaping gap out of its own resources. Exalt your conception of love as of a spirit with a thousand eyes and a thousand hands, and then read anew the words of my text.

"Unto him that loveth us!" "Loveth!" Keen eyes, strong-hearted, strong-handed! What need does He discover, from whom there is nothing concealed? He beholds His children in the bondage of corruption and night. He sees them enslaved by appalling encumbrances that they cannot discard. They are the captives of sin and of death. How has it all arisen? Shall I give you the explanation offered by the apostle James? Here it is. I have a will, most mystic yet most real. This will was purposed by the Almighty to marry the Word of Truth, that out of the pure and gracious union there might arise all the beauties and graces of the divine life.

But, says the apostle James, there comes along a lust, subtle and bewitching. It fastens its fascinating eye upon the will, and the will is enticed. "He is drawn away of his own lust, and enticed." It is a most unholy union and begets a most unholy issue. "Lust, when it hath conceived, beareth sin" (James 1:15), and that is not the end of the awful generation. There is a further offspring—"sin, when it is full-grown, bringeth forth death" (v. 15). Here, then, is the consequence of an immoral union. The soul draws into itself enslaving presences, sin and death, and it cannot shake them away.

The soul is in the bondage of guilt. The soul is in the bondage of death.

Is this an imaginary analysis? Is its basis fictional? One of the clearest and calmest thinkers of our time, a man who sees far into the secret springs of human life, has given his judgment that the most real terrors that afflict men are the guilt of sin and the fear of death. You don't find the evidence of this upon the surface. Men do not like these things to walk abroad, and they seek to bury them in the deepest graves. But the terror is often the most real where the outer life appears undisturbed. It is often the man who is whistling who is most afraid of the ghost.

Do not be misled by the whistle. That is only on the lips, while the terror is shaking the heart. I have heard men speak of their sins, and they could not have spoken about them more jauntily or laughingly if there were no God and no great white throne and no hell! But I have not allowed myself to be deceived. The whistling has been the index to the reality of their fear and not the proof of its absence. Have you never broken into humming and singing to drown the voice of your conscience? Somebody heard you suddenly break into singing, and they interpreted it as a sign of peace and merriment, while all the time its signification was this: a man fighting down his ghosts.

No, do not let us attempt to deceive ourselves. Sin is most real. Guilt is most real. Death is most real. It is not merely the dissolution of the flesh, but that which the gentle Jesus called the "outer darkness" (Matt. 8:12; 22:13; 25:30)—the black night of separation from the holy presence of God. The bondage is most real. How can we obtain deliverance? I want deliverance from the baleful shore of guilt. I want deliverance from the power of acquired habit. I want deliverance from the outer darkness of death. Where can the liberating power be found? I turn to those who have closed the Bible, denouncing its remedies as fictional—or at the best as antique and obsolete—and I ask them what provision they are prepared to put in its place.

The problem is this: Here is a man, guilt-bound, sin-bound, death-bound. Release him. Take that haunted chamber of the mind, lay the ghosts, and make the chamber into a quiet and peaceful living room. Take the heart, and turn out the unclean devils of desire and lust, and tenant it with the white-robed angels of faith and hope and love. Take the evil power out of today, and take the black threat out of tomorrow. That is the problem, often underestimated because the remedies offered are peddling and insufficient. I am not surprised that men who close the Bible would so often interpret human need as though it were a skin complaint and not a heart disease. It is an old device, and you may find the answer to it in the inspired Word, "Though thou wash thee with nitre, and take thee much soap, yet thine iniquity is marked before me, saith the Lord GOD" (Jer. 2:22).

That is a word that, I think, is peculiarly applicable to our own day. Polish is consistent with great depravity. Culture may coexist with rank uncleanness. Sandpaper may smooth a surface, but it cannot change a substance. The primary need of man is not accomplishment but character, and for this we require not the washing of culture, but the washing of regeneration. It is possible to refine away a pimple of uncouthness; it is not possible to refine away guilt. Man can wash himself into good manners; he cannot provide himself with a new heart. When education and culture have reached their utmost limits and the mental powers are refined into exquisite discernment, the two black, gruesome birds of the night remain—guilt and death—and only the Eternal Son can disturb them, and cause them to flee away.

Here, then, there comes in the energetic, sleepless ministry of the Eternal Love. "Unto him that loveth us, and loosed us from our sins by his blood." No man, by his own agony and bloody sweat, could wash his robes and make them white. "*Unto him* that loveth us, and loosed us from our sins by his blood." Is the loosening real? That question does not suggest an argument. I interpret it as a demand for proof. Call for those who are "in Christ," who live in Him by faith, and solicit their testimony. Call the witness and let him declare what the Lord has done for his soul. Let us examine him. What about your ghost chamber, the haunt of paralyzing fears? Has the Lord laid the ghosts? "The peace of God, which passeth all understanding" (Phil. 4:7a) keeps our minds. "He is our peace" (Eph. 2:14a). And how is it with your present temptations, with all the fierce onrush of desire and lust? "We are more than conquerors through him that loved us" (Rom. 8:37). And how about tomorrow and . . . death? "To die is gain" (Phil. 1:21b).

The testimony is eager, persistent, unbroken. The loosening is an immediate and urgent reality. However real may have been the sense of guilt, the driving power of evil inclination, and the chilling fear of judgment, the sense of liberty and reconciliation is even more real, and life exults with a joy unspeakable and full of glory. "Where sin abounded, grace did much more abound: that as sin hath reigned unto death, even so might grace reign through righteousness unto eternal life by Jesus Christ our Lord" (Rom. 5:20b–21). The reality of reconciliation in Christ, of loosening and liberty by His blood, has given the keynote and emphasis to the evangel, which has been the ceaseless glory of this church.

"And he made us to be a kingdom, to be priests unto his God and Father." He "loosed," and then He ennobled. After emancipation there came enfranchisement. We had been in the servitude of the evil one, the poor slaves of an appalling tyranny. Now we are made a kingdom. We become citizens, endowed with a sublime franchise, the possessors of unspeakable privileges and rights. We are made a "kingdom of priests" (Ex. 19:6). Every child has the right to share the sovereignty of Jesus and to enjoy free access into the most secret place of the Father's presence. No longer does He call us "servants . . . but . . . friends" (John 15:15). There is no closed door between us and Him. We have "the run of the house." We may be "at home with the Lord." This is the issue of the primal loving! The ultimate aim of redemption is the creation of a family of sanctified children, reigning as kings and queens in the possession of spiritual powers, and enjoying happy and intimate fellowship with one another and with their Father in heaven.

NOTES

The Vision and Compassion of Jesus

John Daniel Jones (1865–1942) served for forty years at the Richmond Hill Congregational Church in Bournemouth, England, where he ministered the Word with a remarkable consistency of quality and effectiveness, as his many volumes of published sermons attest. A leader in his denomination, he gave himself to church extension (he helped to start thirty new churches), assistance to needier congregations, and increased salaries for the clergy. He spoke at D. L. Moody's Northfield Bible Conference in 1919.

This sermon was taken from his book *The Gospel of the Sovereignty,* reprinted in 1914 by Hodder and Stoughton.

John Daniel Jones

9

THE VISION AND COMPASSION OF JESUS

But when he saw the multitudes, he was moved with compassion for them, because they were distressed and scattered, as sheep not having a shepherd (Matthew 9:36 ASV).

THE MAIN VERB of my text is that which is translated "he was moved with compassion," and that main verb sets forth the main positive statement of the verse. To that main statement I intend to devote the greater part of my sermon. In other words, the subject I mean to preach about is the "compassion of Christ." But the grammatical structure of my text makes it quite clear that the compassion was the result of something else. "When he saw the multitudes, he was moved with compassion"; or, to translate the Greek sentence quite literally, "Having seen . . . he was moved with compassion." The one thing was the consequence of the other. His pity sprang from His perception. His compassion was the result of His vision.

The Vision of Christ

And that is the first thing about which I wish to speak with you—the *vision of Christ*. It was the condition antecedent of His compassion. "He saw the multitudes." You may tell me there is nothing at all extraordinary about that. Anybody who has two eyes in his head can see a crowd when there is a crowd to be seen. But can he? That is the very point. If seeing depends simply on the possession of two sound eyes, how is it people see so differently? How is it the very same sights produce such differing impressions? How is it that to Peter Bell "a primrose by the river's brim, a yellow primrose is to him, and it is nothing more," while to Wordsworth the meanest flower that blew had power in it to quicken thoughts that did often lie too deep for tears? How is it that to some people, as Mrs. Barrett Browning puts it, "earth's crammed with heaven, and every common bush afire with God," while the rest see no gleam of fire in the bush, but simply sit around it and eat blackberries? How is it that when the sun rises some people see just a disc of fire something like a guinea, but a poet-painter like Blake sees an "innumerable company of the heavenly host crying, 'Holy, Holy, Holy is the Lord God, the Almighty' (Rev. 4:8)"? Nothing could be shallower or falser than to suggest that what we see depends upon these two eyes of ours, and that, if our eyes are equally good, one will see as much as the other.

Away back in the days of my childhood I can remember a reading lesson entitled "Eyes, and No Eyes," which told of two schoolboys and a country walk they took. And to one the walk had been full of wonders and glories and surprises, while to the other it had been dull and boring because he had seen nothing at all. And long before that writer wrote his sketch Jesus spoke of people who, though they had eyes to see, did not *perceive*.

The fact is, vision is not a faculty of the physical organ of sight solely. What a man sees depends not simply on his eye, but on his mind, his imagination, his heart. A man may have eyes, sound and perfect in every particular, but unless he has also an imagination and a heart to look out through those eyes, he will not perceive.

Now the secret of our Lord's vision was this: He looked out upon the world with imagination and a perfect sympathy. He not only *saw,* He *perceived.* And that is why, when He *saw* the multitudes, He was "moved with compassion." If it were true that everyone blessed with two sound eyes saw alike, then the sight of the crowd ought to have produced the same impression upon all who saw it. The twelve disciples were with Jesus at this time, but I do not read that any one of them was "moved with compassion." I read it only of Jesus. And I read it only of Jesus because, in the deepest sense of all, He was the only One who saw the crowd. The rest saw heads, faces, bodies, numbers. Jesus was the only One who truly and really "saw the multitudes."

Now, my friends, even to the dullest and most prosaic of men there is something impressive, inspiring, subduing in the sight of a great crowd. What preacher is there, for instance, who is not acquainted with the inspiration that comes from numbers? When the multitudes press upon the preacher to hear the Word of God, he is uplifted, exalted, clean carried out of himself. And it is possibly this inspiring and encouraging effect of the multitude that is the most familiar effect. In numbers we see power. But to the man who looks out with imagination and sympathy the crowd supplies not only ground for exultation, it supplies also abundant food for tears. You remember the old story of Xerxes reviewing his troops before they crossed the Hellespont to invade Greece. As they marched past in seemingly endless regiments and battalions, the monarch's first feeling was one of swelling pride. In these numberless thousands of soldiers he saw the evidence and expression of measureless power. Then another feeling seized him. He remembered that of all these multitudes in a hundred years' time there would not be one left, and Xerxes on his throne burst out into a transport of tears. He had seen his multitudes not only in the pomp of their power, but as the prey of death.

And the remembrance that all are doomed to die is not the only thought that stirs one to sadness as one gazes upon a crowd. What disappointments, what sorrows, what heartbreaks a crowd represents! If we only knew everything about one another, what tragedies would be revealed even in this morning's congregation! "The heart knoweth its own bitterness," the old Book says (Prov. 14:10). And every heart, well-near, has its bitterness. Business trouble, blighted affections, bereavement, the sorrow and shame caused by sin—they are represented in every crowd. The vision of it all in its naked horror would be more than flesh and blood could bear. It is in mercy that God has, in part at any rate, veiled it from our eyes.

But Jesus "*saw* the multitudes." He saw not only their faces, He saw their hearts. "He . . . knew what was in man," John says (John 2:25). His "kind but searching glance could scan the very wounds that shame would hide." He walked through life with a vision to which everything was unveiled. That was why, on occasion, He gave way to emotions that startled and amazed the bystanders. "When he drew nigh, he saw the city and wept over it" (Luke 19:41). The bursting of Jerusalem on the view was for most pilgrims an occasion for rejoicing and shouts of gladness. But He, when He saw the city, wept over it. The fact was, He was the only One who saw the city. The others saw Jerusalem's temple and its palaces. Jesus saw Jerusalem's people and their sin and their tragic doom. He was the only One who wept because He was the only One who saw. This was one reason why Jesus was a man of sorrows and acquainted with grief. He saw, as no one else ever saw, the pain and sin and woe of the world.

And this is why I read in my text that Jesus having seen "the multitudes . . . was moved with compassion." His disciples saw the numbers of people who gathered around their Lord, and their feeling was one of elation. In these thronging multitudes they saw new recruits for their Master's cause. A growing army—that was what the disciples saw, and they rejoiced. A multitude of men and women bowed down beneath burdens of care and sorrow and sin—that was what Jesus saw, and He was stirred to a passion of pity for them. "When he *saw* the multitudes, he was moved with compassion."

And before I pass on, I want to make this remark: *Vision is still the condition of compassion.* There is a vast amount of apathy and unconcern and callousness in our modern society. I tell you quite frankly, I do not believe that people could go on living in selfish and wanton luxury, for instance, if they once really saw the need and misery all about them. They are indifferent to the cruel wrongs of life because they do not see them. I admit that there are some people so innately selfish that they do not want to see, and, if they can possibly avoid it, they will not see. They do not want their peace of mind disturbed;

they do not want their consciences aroused. They are like that Persian king who would not allow anyone in sackcloth to come near his palace for fear he would be reminded that there was such a thing as death in the world.

I read an American novel last year entitled *V. V.'s Eyes*. It was about a girl who did not know, and for a long time did not want to know, anything about the condition of those whose labor procured her comfort and her wealth. There *are* some hard and selfish natures, let us admit it, who simply do not want to see or know. But there are multitudes more who are indifferent and unconcerned just because they are ignorant. They have never seen the multitude, and so they go on their way heedless and uncaring. What we need in order to stir us up to service and sacrifice and something of our Lord's redeeming passion is *a clarified vision*. We want to *see* the multitude.

I said a moment ago that it is in mercy that God has drawn a veil over our eyes so that we cannot see all the ghastly tragedy of human souls. And yet I want to go on now to say that the more we see, the more we seek to see, the more like Christ we become. It is a painful knowledge, I am aware. But the Christian is one who enters into "the fellowship of [Christ's] sufferings" (Phil. 3:10). He is one who is willing to share Christ's sorrows. Therefore, if we are really anxious to be like Christ, we shall make it our business to try to *see*. We shall bring ourselves face to face with the tragic facts of life. When we see men we shall think of the burdens, cares, and sorrows they carry. We shall train ourselves to see the multitudes as Christ saw them. We shall think not only of their circumstances, but also of their souls. And seeing them so—seeing them in their want and need and sin— we too, like Jesus, shall be "moved with compassion," and that compassion in turn will inspire us with our Lord's passion for service. A clarified vision is the condition of an enlarged compassion.

The Compassion of Christ

And now, having spoken of the vision, let me speak of the *compassion* that issued from it. "When he saw the multitudes, he was moved with compassion." That word *compassion* is a rich and beautiful word, and it exactly describes the feelings of Christ when He beheld the multitude. It derives from the Latin and is compounded of two words that mean literally "suffering with." And that is exactly what Jesus did when He came across need and distress and pain. "He suffered with" them. He felt the distress and pain as if it were His own. In all their afflictions He was afflicted. He bore their griefs and carried their sorrows. He "suffered with" all sufferers.

Now there is a sort of "sweet monotony," as Dr. Kilpatrick says, in the way in which this grace of compassion is attributed to Christ in the Gospels. He had a perfect passion for helping, healing, saving. There was not a single ill under which men suffered that Jesus did not "suffer with" them. Three things especially called out Christ's compassion. I mention them in their ascending order: (1) physical need, (2) pain and sorrow, (3) the ruin and havoc caused by sin. The sight of these things always "moved him to compassion."

He was moved with compassion for *physical want and need*. "I have compassion on the multitude," He said one day, "because they continue with me now three days, and have nothing to eat" (Matt. 15:32). The sight of the world's poor always stirred our Lord's soul to pity. He Himself knew, I imagine, the pinch of poverty. There had not been much to spare in the little home at Nazareth. And He had Himself endured the pangs of hunger. Our Lord was always "moved with compassion" at the sight of fainting and famished people. I need not protest to you that Christ's primary business is with man's soul. He came to seek and to save the lost. He was essentially and principally not a social reformer, but a Savior. But I should be giving a totally false impression of our Lord if I implied or allowed you to infer that He had no concern for the bodies of men. Christ cared not only for men's spiritual condition, but also for the external circumstances under which they lived. He came to preach good tidings to the poor. His own heart was stirred to its depths by the sight of need. And His sternest warnings were addressed to men who, like Dives, neglected the poor who were at their gates.

The Christian is bound, like his Lord, "to consider the poor." To reduce Christianity to a sort of program of social reform is a grave error on the one side, but to say it has nothing to do with social reform is to be guilty of as grave an error on the other. *The poor are our concern.* The fact that millions of our own countrymen are living on the poverty line—that is our concern. The fact that children grow up in our midst who are sent forth into life crippled and maimed because they are not adequately fed and clothed—that is our concern. The fact that there are people so badly paid for their labor that they cannot marry, or if they marry, cannot maintain their families in decency—that is our concern. The wrongs of the poor touched the fountains of Christ's pity. We are no followers of His unless the vision of those same wrongs stirs us up also to compassion. And Christianity itself is a make-believe unless, wherever it is professed, it means good tidings to the poor.

Our Lord was "moved with compassion" by the vision of *pain and sorrow*. He "suffered with" every sufferer. It was from this infinite compassion of His for pain and suffering that nearly all His deeds of power sprang. His miracles were the product of His pity. A leper came to Him and besought Him to set him free from his loathsome disease. Jesus, "moved with compassion," stretched forth His hand and said, "I will; be thou clean" (Matt. 8:3).

Two men sat by the wayside at Jericho begging. The crowd tried to silence them when they began to cry out to Jesus for healing. But He commanded them to be brought, and "moved with compassion" (Matt. 20:34) for these men who were shut out from the vision of God's fair earth and the sight of their own beloved, He touched their eyes and "straightway they received their sight" (v. 34).

He was walking into Nain one day and at the gate He met a funeral. It was the funeral of a young man who was the only son of his mother, and she a widow! It was a common enough sight, I dare say. But the pathos of it all touched our Lord's heart. He "suffered with" that weeping mother. "When the Lord saw her, he had compassion on her, and said unto her, Weep not. And he came and touched the bier. . . . And he said, Young man, I say unto thee, Arise. And he that was dead sat up. . . . And he delivered him to his mother" (Luke 7:13–15).

Our Lord was moved with compassion for the poor. He was stirred to a still profounder pity for the suffering and the sorrow-stricken. Pain and loss are more tragic evils even than poverty, and our Lord was always quick to minister to them. And whosoever would be a Christian must be like his Lord in this respect—he must have compassion on every wounded man he comes across along life's way.

And he must be on the lookout for the wounded man, too. The world is full of grief and loss. Do you constrain yourselves sometimes to think of it? We see the halt and the lame and the blind in our streets. Do you feel the throb of sympathy when you pass them, and does your sympathy sometimes prompt you to say a kind word? We have our hospitals and homes in every town. Do you ever think of the sufferers who lie on the beds and fill the wards? Do you ever think of the men lying there weak and helpless, unable to win bread for their families? Do you ever think of the mothers lying there, separated from their children? Do you ever think of the little children lying there cut off from the frolic and play of childhood? What burdens these people carry! Is your heart ever moved with compassion as you think of them?

Occasionally as you go about your daily business you meet a funeral. Does the sight of one ever melt you to tears? Do you ever think of the desolate hearts in the carriages as they pass? We live in a world of bleeding and broken hearts. And while, perhaps, compassion cannot heal disease or snatch the prey from the jaws of death, for bleeding and broken hearts it is a sovereign balm. If we want to imitate Christ, that is the first thing we must do—we must put on a "heart of compassion."

And thirdly, our Lord was "moved with compassion"

by the vision of the *havoc and ruin wrought by sin.* That was what stirred Him to such a passion of pity as He looked forth on the multitudes referred to in my text. It is quite possible that the majority of them belonged to the peasant class. But it was not the thought of their poverty that so deeply moved Christ. And it was not that there were many sick in the crowd. It was the ordinary, everyday, normal sort of multitude. What moved Christ with compassion was their moral condition. They were like sheep not having a shepherd. They had wandered away from the pastures and had gotten lost. And once deprived of the shepherd's oversight and care, they had become exposed to all sorts of perils and disasters. They were "distressed and scattered." That was the vision Christ had of this multitude. To the everyday onlooker they were just a crowd of average, respectable, decent men and women. Jesus, who knew what was in man, saw them as distressed and scattered sheep.

They were "distressed." The English word does not adequately convey the force of the Greek word which it translates. The Greek word means literally "flayed, torn, mangled." What usually happened to a sheep that went astray was that it fell a prey to prowling beasts who tore and mangled it. And that was how Jesus beheld the people in this crowd—they were flayed, torn, and mangled by sin. "The devil, as a roaring lion, walketh about, seeking whom he may devour," says Peter (1 Peter 5:8). And the souls of these people had been among the lions. They bore the marks of the lions' claws and teeth upon them. They were lacerated, flayed, torn. They were full of wounds and bruises and festering sores. Upon their honor, their truth, their purity, their good name the lion had laid his claws. And from many a wounded spirit the cry was going up to God, "Save me from the lion's mouth" (Ps. 22:21).

And they were not only "flayed and torn," but "scattered" too. And again that word "scattered" scarcely does justice to the Greek. Literally the word means "thrown down," "prostrate," either through faintness or famine. It is a picture of a sheep at the last gasp, unable to rise for weakness. And that again is how Jesus beheld the people in the crowd—trampled down, prostrate, unable to rise—"sick, and ready to die" (Luke 7:2). For that again is what sin does to men. It not only tears and mangles men, it tramples on them. It reduces them to helplessness and despair. It robs them of the power to rise. Sin means disablement as well as disfigurement. And the disablement, unless rescue comes, is bound to end in death. The prostrate sheep is bound to be the wild beast's prey. And that is how Jesus saw the people—torn and prostrate, disfigured and disabled, and in consequent danger of death through sin. "But when he saw the multitudes, he was moved with compassion for them, because they were distressed and scattered, as sheep not having a shepherd."

Nothing moved Christ to such pity as the vision of sin. Poverty and pain, in our Lord's view, were not to be nearly so much dreaded as sin. The power for mischief of poverty and pain is limited; sin's power for evil seems infinite and eternal. Poverty and pain for the most part affect the body, but sin menaces the immortal soul. Therefore, primarily, Jesus Christ came into the world to save His people from their sins. He came to rescue those people who had been drawn aside by their own lusts and enticed. And because He could not rescue them in any easier way, He gave Himself to the wild beasts. He who knew no sin became sin for us. He allowed sin's claws and fangs to fall on Him that the poor, flayed, and prostrate sheep might escape. "The good shepherd giveth his life for the sheep" (John 10:11).

And whoever would be a Christian must, like his Lord, be "moved with compassion" at the sight of the havoc and ruin wrought by sin. But here comes in one of the most astonishing facts of the modern situation: men and women have become sensitive about poverty and pain, but careless and indifferent about sin. They are more affected by sickness of body than they are by sickness of soul. Philanthropy has become more fashionable than religion. People give far more readily and easily to hospitals than they do to missions. The reason for this is that they do not see the multitudes as Jesus saw them. They see the external mischief, but they do not see the deadly secret hurt. And that is what we want for a revival of our evangelic zeal, for a recovery of the lost "passion for souls." We want to see the people as Jesus saw them. If we saw the people in foreign lands as Jesus saw them, if we saw the indifferent and godless multitude at home as Jesus saw them, we would see them as lost sheep, mangled and prostrate sheep, sheep at the very point of death. For that is exactly what they are. Sin rends and tears and defiles and destroys the soul. We are callous and indifferent and unconcerned just because we do not see. You remember the lines F. W. H. Myers puts into Paul's lips? He is describing the people to whom he preached:

> Only like souls I see the folk thereunder,
> > Bound who should conquer, slaves who
> > should be kings,
> Hearing their one hope with an empty
> > wonder,
> > Sadly contented with a show of things.
>
> Then with a rush the intolerable craving
> > Shivers throughout me like a trumpet call,
> Oh, to save these, to perish for their saving,
> > Die for their life, be offered for them all.

And if we *saw,* we too would share with Christ the work of seeking the lost and would be willing to become all things to all men, if we could by all means save some.

The Love of God

Adoniram Judson Gordon (1836–1895) pastored the
Clarendon Street Baptist Church in Boston from 1869
to 1895 and boldly preached the orthodox faith while
many pulpiteers were yielding to the "new truths" of
evolution and "higher criticism." He was a vigorous
promoter of missions and prophetic teaching, and his
ministry led to the founding of Gordon College and
Gordon-Conwell Seminary.

This sermon was taken from *The Great Pulpit
Masters: A. J. Gordon,* published in 1951 by Fleming
H. Revell.

Adoniram Judson Gordon

10

THE LOVE OF GOD

The Son of God, who loved me, and gave himself for me
(Galatians 2:20c).

SOME OF US never get beyond the vague notion of a
benevolent power working in and through the world,
which somehow overrules all things for good. The above
text expresses a more satisfying viewpoint as it sets forth
the love of God in Jesus Christ. It reminds us that that
love is individual. "Who loved me"—we could never be
content with a love that had no focus. A good will that is
so infinitely diffused that it touches everywhere in
general and fails to touch anywhere in particular is no
more than an ineffectual sentiment. Yet just here lies the
difference between that "eternal goodness," so much on
the lips of sentimental religionists, and the personal love
for individual souls which the Gospel declares to us.

Love is a real, measurable, comprehensible thing. A
ray of light can be analyzed. It is composed of several
distinct and recognizable colors—red, violet, orange, and
the rest. So love can be resolved into its constituents and
shown to include such elements as sympathy, yearning,
and goodwill. If these do not show themselves, we may
conclude we are dealing with something else than real
love. How is it with the benevolence we seem to find in
nature? Is it sufficient to meet the needs of the human
heart? We look up into the starry firmament at night and
are powerfully reminded of God's wisdom and majesty.
But so far from finding in it any suggestion of divine
sympathy, such vastness quite excludes this from our
thought. We are affected as was David: "When I consider
thy heavens, the work of thy fingers, the moon and the
stars, which thou hast ordained, what is man, that thou
art mindful of him?" (Ps. 8:3–4a). The heavens suggest

the diffuseness of God's benevolence. For they stoop down impartially over the barest plain and the most squalid hut at night with all the stellar magnificence that they shed upon the blooming garden and the marble palace. But the discrimination and individuality so essential to personal love are absent.

The opening flower, again, with the exquisite tinting of leaf and petal, and the delicious fragrance that drops from its cup, witnesses to divine goodwill but never suggests compassion for me in my sin or sympathy with me in my sorrows and struggles. If we are looking for a basis for our piety, this defect is radical. A love that is not specific and personal can never meet man's deeper spiritual cravings. A love that cannot in its last analysis be reduced to an individual regard for *me*—and a pity for *me,* and a goodwill toward *me,* and a willingness to suffer and sacrifice for *me*—is not the love that my soul longs for and requires.

This truth is illustrated in our relations with each other. A young man is said, in popular language, to "fall in love" with a girl. That means that he cherishes for her a special affection and partiality. Philanthropy could never be a sufficient ground for marriage. A general goodwill and kindliness toward the human race would never serve as strong enough motive for being joined in wedlock to some member of that race. Conjugal love must be individual and exclusive, or it will never warrant the sympathies and toils and sacrifices which the marriage relationship involves.

So with the love of God in Jesus Christ. It is infinitely general, and yet at the same time intensely specific. It is like the sun that fills the whole earth with its radiance and warmth, and yet mirrors itself in luminous fullness in each dewdrop. It embraces all creation in its compass, and yet concentrates itself with direct and, as it were, undivided ardor upon each separate soul. "God so loved the world, that he gave his only begotten Son" (John 3:16). "Who loved *me* and gave himself for *me.*"

No single one of us, therefore, shall ever say in the world to come that he was left orphaned and unloved, that in the breadth and diffuseness of the divine affection it failed to compass one poor sinner. Many a guilty transgressor may utter the complaint and justly say: "No man cared for my soul" (Ps. 142:4b). But none can truly say: "The Christ who loved the world and died for the world forgot me in His salvation and lost sight of me among the multitude of the subjects of His grace." Christ's love can miss no one. A minuteness of regard which numbers each hair of our heads can never overlook an immortal soul amid the myriads of creation. So be assured, O sinner, that however vast be the boundaries of your Savior's love, it is a love that keeps sight of *you,* and goes out to *you,* and yearns for *you* in *your* disobedience, just as if there were no other in all His universe.

I have already suggested that love may be analyzed and shown to include such elements as pity, kindliness, self-denial. The cross is the prism that accomplishes this wondrous analysis. The love of God shining through the cross in white, unbroken ray emerges from it revealed in all these lovely hues of "manifold," or as the word means exactly, "many-colored," grace. Through the cross we see divine compassion—love yearning for the miserable; divine forgiveness—love going out to the unworthy and sinful; and divine self-sacrifice—love giving itself for the lost. So, on the cross the often repeated declaration of Scripture that Christ loved us is translated into the most familiar of all dialect—that of human suffering. Thus the true measure of that "*so* loved the world" is furnished in the gift of Him who cared enough to die for the world.

"[He] loved me." "[He] gave himself for me." It is no part of Himself or His possessions, such as we give lightly and call self-denial, and not some precious fragment broken off and flung into the fire of sacrifice. That word "self" expresses as strongly as is possible the wholeness of being. It is the integer of our humanity which cannot be increased. And this He gave—for *me.* Shall so much of divine pity and loving-kindness and sacrifice directed toward me not warm me from the torpor of indifference?

Shall I lie directly in the focus of eternal love and be so encased in hardness and frozen with unbelief that its genial rays shall utterly fail to penetrate my heart?

"Love so amazing, so divine" deserves my truest, tenderest devotion in return. His love measured itself by His sacrifice. "[He] loved me and gave *himself* for me." And if there is any who can rise to that high level of argument, he will say: "Even so I love and give myself to Him." Christ does not ask that our love should be equal to His. But He does ask that it shall be equal to ourselves. He made Himself the measure of His love. We are bound accordingly to make ourselves the measure of our love—and give *ourselves.* "And that he died for all, that they which live should not henceforth live unto themselves, but unto him which died for them, and rose again" (2 Cor. 5:15).

Keep Yourselves in the Love of God (Jude 21)

We are not told to keep ourselves in love with God, or to keep the love of God in ourselves. That might be impossible, for love is hard to control. We may do our best to incite our affections, to kindle our hearts into fervor, to exercise strong aspiration toward God. But with all this we may be constantly failing to advance in the divine love. A shipmaster says: "Sailing from Cuba we thought we had gained sixty miles in our course one day, but at the next observation we found we had lost more than thirty miles. The ship had been going forward by the wind but going backward by the current." The experience of the soul may be similar. While there is great activity in pushing ahead in Christian work, strong religious emotions, powerful spiritual exercises, we may be retrogressing all the while because, though our sails are set for the gales of heaven, our keel dips into the undercurrent of the world. So the question becomes not how we feel, or how we "enjoy our mind," as the saying is, or how much inner satisfaction or ecstasy we experience, but how deeply we are in communion with God.

Nothing is more difficult to estimate than our personal experiences. How much of our love is artificially generated? How much of our enjoyment is the effervescence of good spirits? How much of our happy feeling is merely self-stimulated excitement? These things are difficult to determine. So God does not set us to careful examination of our spiritual frames and feelings. The eye of faith, like the eye of the body, looks outward, not inward. If we turn it within, the consequent light may be only the stimulated flash of the optic nerve. Our emotions, that is to say, may be largely the result of our physical states. What we call "religious depression," when we look back upon it, may prove to have been due to the damps and vapors of bodily sickness that were clouding the soul. So some period of rare spiritual elevation may be traceable to an unusually high tide in the ebbing and flowing of our physical health. We would emphasize, therefore, the importance of drinking constantly at the eternal fountain as the only way we may be sure of a well within us "springing up into everlasting life" (John 4:14).

Our temptation is to reverse God's order, to let the action be from self toward God instead of from God toward self. I sometimes think that the same ambition which leads men to strive for originality in thought leads them to strive for originality in spiritual things. They wish to be givers instead of receivers. "Genius," somebody has said, "is the ability to light one's own fire." The ability, that is, to strike off ideas which nobody has expressed before. And we think to be geniuses in religion and produce sparks of love and devotion which draw the eye of God toward ourselves. But God is the true originator. "We love him, because he first loved us" (1 John 4:19). Our affections are but the resultant and return of His. Let us see to it that we receive before we attempt to give.

We have five senses that bring us into communication with the external world. We have only to open our eyes that our whole body may be full of light. We have only to open our ears that our whole body may be full of melody. Strange folly would it be to close the eyelid and try to get light by exciting the optic nerve to give out flashes of fire, or to close the ear to external harmonies and try to get music in the soul by some artificial vibration of the eardrums. And shall we seek to quicken our love by working up our emotions? That may result in flashes of ecstasy and scintillations of enthusiasm. But for the love that endures, that keeps on in calm, growing, and deepening exercise, we have simply to open the soul to God, and take in all the rich and abundant manifestations of His love that He has given us in the person of Christ and in the revelation of the Word. A single hour's study of the New Testament, a single hour's contemplation of the suffering and sacrifice of Jesus Christ will do more to help us in our purpose to love the Lord our God than months and years of introspection and heart manipulation.

Acquaint Now Thyself with Him [God], and Be at Peace (Job 22:21a)

Remember that acquaintance can come through no casual contact: Calling on God in the morning and leaving our visiting card of devotion, but having no care as to whether we find Him at home and really catch sight of His face; talking with God through an interpreter, through the minister or the sacraments or the hymnbook—but knowing nothing of real and intimate and personal conversation with Him. This is not acquaintance with God. It is a kind of society etiquette like that which requires that we be polite to our neighbors even when we have no real interest in them. Beware of formalism. It is the decorum of religion. And what will it avail, though we be deeply skilled therein, if we know not what it is to have "fellowship . . . with the Father, and with his Son Jesus Christ" (1 John 1:3b)? What earnest prayer, what profound meditation upon the Word, what chastening of the inward and the outward cross there must be in order that we may truly be acquainted with God. The sweetest expositions of Scripture are, for this reason, found in lives rather than in learned books.

I Will Bear the Indignation of the Lord (Micah 7:9a)

Do not imagine that because God blots out transgressions He therefore blots out the distinction between right and wrong, between good and evil, between sin and holiness. "The sin of Judah is written with a pen of iron and with the point of a diamond," says Scripture (Jer. 17:1). God uses the graving tool to emphasize the reality of evil as well as the eraser to obliterate the penalties thereof. And while the Gospel sweeps the tablet of our life with one blessed text: "The blood of Jesus Christ his Son cleanseth us from all sin" (1 John 1:7b), it also uncovers the handwriting of the law, deep-graven and ineffaceable, "The wages of sin is death" (Rom. 6:23a) and "sin is the transgression of the law" (1 John 3:4b).

If one expects the mercy of God, he must put himself under the law of God. He must say, "I have sinned," and submit himself to the consequences of sin, the indignation of the Lord. And there is no one who does not deserve that indignation in view of our selfishness, our sinfulness, our love of the present world, and our forgetfulness of God. If for one hour we could see ourselves as God sees us, if the untempered light of His uncovered face could be let in upon us, there could be no escaping His judgment. We have sometimes turned up a stone in a field just to see the nameless brood of hideous insects underneath as they rushed in every direction to hide themselves from the revealing sun. So if the shield of respectability were suddenly removed, if the sanction of false custom were lifted, if human palliations and excuses were taken away, and our hearts were left open and naked before Him with whom we have to do, what a hurrying and hiding there would be from the face of Him that sits on the throne! What a shrinking away of secret sins, of enmity and jealousy and falsehood and impurity! In these days of shallow theology there is nothing more needful than frequent days of thorough self-examination. We ought now and again to take out a search warrant for our own hearts, and as we come to know the evil that is in us say: "Strike, Lord, for I deserve the worst. I will not evade. I will not extenuate. I will not contend. 'I will bear the indignation of the Lord, because I have sinned against him' (Micah 7:9a)."

But . . . Afterward (Heb. 12:11b)

It is possible for a man to get a blessing even out of a sinful past. He who can strike the lowest note in the scale of regret can often strike the highest note in the scale of exultation. It was because Paul knew himself the "chief of sinners" that he was able to lift his voice so high in praise of Christ, "the chief among ten thousand, the one altogether lovely." "The sting of death is sin," writes Paul (1 Cor. 15:56a). We may say that sin is equally the sting of life. For the memory of wrong-doing is the one and only thing that can make us miserable in life and death alike. But if that remembrance of sin be accompanied with the remembrance of mercy, so that we can say, "Where sin abounded, grace did much more abound" (Rom. 5:20b), it may become the source of unspeakable joy.

It has been discovered that the sting of a bee has purposes other than pain for its enemies. When the cell is filled with pure honey and the lid is finished, a drop of formic acid from the poison bag connected with the sting is added to the honey by perforating the lid. This formic acid preserves the honey from fermentation. Most insects that have a stinging apparatus like that of the bee are collectors and storers of honey. How blessed the parable here! As often as my guilty past comes before me and sin thrusts its sting into my conscience, I see that this is only to keep the honey of grace sweet and pure, making me love much because I am forgiven much. O memory, drive the sting of sin deep into my heart, and I shall cry out: "Yes, I have sinned; but the blood of Jesus Christ His Son cleanseth us from all sin." O Accuser of Christians, remind me if you will that the sting of death is sin. I will appeal to the Advocate of the brethren on high, saying, "If we confess our sins, he is faithful and just to forgive us our sins, and to cleanse us from all unrighteousness" (1 John 1:9). There is nothing that can keep the honey of assurance so sweet as the thrusts of sin's envenomed sting.

Ye Who Love the Lord, Hate Evil (Ps. 97:10a)

There are both attractions and repulsions in Christian love. It is capable not only of warming and comforting, but also, when raised to its highest temperature, of burning and destroying. The Christian love that always keeps a medium temperature where it delights in God and His attributes is not all that is required. God wants a love that will burn up sin in us as well as warm our religious affections. We ought to shudder and shrink from sin as we instinctively do from a serpent, which we hasten to bruise under our heel. Is there anything more repulsive than the serpent charmer who has deliberately schooled himself to fondle snakes, carrying them in his bosom and letting them twine about his neck? But there are professed Christians who treat sins in the same way, and learn to live on good terms with them. Some learn to live in covetousness, some in worldly fashion, some in self-indulgence. They become so accustomed to these things that they result in no pangs of conscience.

There are two classes of sins that we are most likely to encounter: indulgence of things forbidden and excessive use of things permitted. True Christians may fall into either, but no Christian can remain in either happy, content, satisfied. We all of us tend to a more or less fixed condition. We are becoming inured to sin so that it sits easily on our conscience, or we are becoming assimilated to holiness so that sin hurts and discomforts us. Our condition is determined by the relative strength of the two elements. Water will quench fire, or fire will quench water according to which is stronger. A pail of water on a little fire will put it out, but a powerful flame on a little water will evaporate and dissipate it. So if the fire of Christian love is strong and steady it will quench our besetting sin, but if the love of the world be dominant in us it will quench the Spirit.

Blessed be God for the Gospel of His Son with its provision not only for forgiving but for destroying sin. Lifted up, He draws all men to Him, but in His drawing He separates. As the ray of sunlight falling upon a muddy pool draws up a clear and crystalline drop of water and leaves behind the soil that was mingled with it, so Christ draws the sinner out of his sin, His love repelling the evil at the same time that it attracts the evildoer. In this He is our example. We should love God and lost souls for whom He gave His Son, while with great vehemence we hate the sin that nailed Him to the cross.

Who . . . hath translated us into the kingdom of his dear Son (Col. 1:13)

God deals first of all with persons. He forgives the sinner, not the sin; He changes the man, not his clothes. He translates us into the kingdom. This needs emphasis because there is so much second-hand dealing with the Lord, through creeds and conduct and covenant, while the soul holds off from Him and stands on its own ground. "I believe in Christ," says one, "but I make no profession." So he uses his faith as he does his opera glasses, to seem to be near the Lord while he is far from Him. So with those who contribute of their means to the church though otherwise they hold themselves aloof. We seek not yours but "you," says the apostle.

A man's weight is in his personality, not in his property. And the Lord requires the weight of our influence to be thrown into His cause. A man's weight can never be known if he has one foot on the scales and the other on the floor. So we cannot estimate your real moral and spiritual heft and register it on God's side, so long as you have one foot in the world and the other in the church. Think of this and don't delay longer to identify yourself definitely with God's people. He does not want you to stay out and give in your influence and your contributions to the church, but to come within and give out your influence and blessing to the world. The kingdom of God ought to be the radiating center from which your life should shed forth blessings instead of a circumference on which you touch only casually and occasionally.

NOTES

Love: The Greatest Thing in the World

Henry Drummond (1851–1897) was trained as an instructor in natural science and taught in his native Scotland, eventually becoming professor at the Free Church College, Glasgow. Influenced by Dwight L. Moody, Drummond developed into an effective personal worker and evangelist to the students, and was greatly used to win many to Christ. He is best known for this address on 1 Corinthians 13, "Love: The Greatest Thing in the World."

This sermon was taken from *The Greatest Thing in the World and Other Addresses,* published in 1898 by Fleming H. Revell Company. Kregel Publications has released an expanded version of Drummond's work on 1 Corinthians 13 by Lewis Drummond.

Henry Drummond

11

LOVE: THE GREATEST
THING IN THE WORLD

If I speak with the tongues of men and of angels, and
have not love, I am become sounding brass, or a clanging
cymbal. And if I have the gift of prophecy, and know all
mysteries and all knowledge; and if I have all faith, so
as to remove mountains, but have not love, I am nothing.
And if I bestow all my goods to feed the poor, and if I
give my body to be burned, but have not love, it profiteth
me nothing.

Love suffereth long, and is kind; love envieth not; love
vaunteth not itself, is not puffed up, doth not behave
itself unseemly, seeketh not its own, is not provoked,
taketh not account of evil; rejoiceth not in
unrighteousness, but rejoiceth with the truth; beareth
all things, believeth all things, hopeth all things,
endureth all things.

Love never faileth: but whether there be prophecies, they
shall be done away; whether there be tongues, they shall
cease; whether there be knowledge, it shall be done away.
For we know in part, and we prophesy in part: but when
that which is perfect is come, that which is in part shall
be done away.

When I was a child, I spake as a child, I felt as a child, I
thought as a child: now that I am became a man, I have
put away childish things. For now we see in a mirror,
darkly; but then face to face: now I know in part; but
then shall I know even as also I have been known.

But now abideth faith, hope, love, these three; and the
greatest of these is love (1 Corinthians 13 RV).

EVERYONE HAS ASKED himself the great question of
antiquity as of the modern world: What is the *summum
bonum*—the supreme good? You have life before you.
Once only you can live it. What is the noblest object of
desire, the supreme gift to covet?

We have been told that the greatest thing in the
religious world is faith. That great word has been the

keynote for centuries of the popular religion. We have easily learned to look upon it as the greatest thing in the world. Well, we are wrong. If we have been told that, we may miss the mark. In 1 Corinthians 13, Paul takes us to *Christianity at its source*. There we see, "The greatest of these is love" (v. 13).

It is not an oversight. Paul was speaking of faith just a moment before. He says, "If I have all faith, so that I can remove mountains, and have not love, I am nothing." So far from forgetting, he deliberately contrasts them, "Now abideth faith, hope, love" (v. 13), and without a moment's hesitation the decision falls, "The greatest of these is love."

And it is not prejudice. A man is apt to recommend to others his own strong point. Love was not Paul's strong point. The observing student can detect a beautiful tenderness growing and ripening all through his character as Paul gets old. But the hand that wrote, "The greatest of these is love," when we meet it first, is stained with blood.

Nor is this letter to the Corinthians peculiar in singling out love as the *summum bonum*. The masterpieces of Christianity are agreed about it. Peter says, "Above all things being fervent in your love among yourselves" (1 Peter 4:8). *Above all things*. And John goes further, "God is love" (1 John 4:8).

You remember the profound remark that Paul makes elsewhere, "Love . . . is the fulfilment of the law" (Rom. 13:10). Did you ever think what he meant by that? In those days men were working the passage to heaven by keeping the Ten Commandments, and the hundred and ten other commandments that they had manufactured out of them. Christ came and said, "I will show you a more simple way. If you do one thing, you will do these hundred and ten things, without ever thinking about them. If you *love*, you will unconsciously fulfill the whole law."

You can readily see for yourselves how that must be so. Take any of the commandments. "Thou shalt have no other gods before me" (Ex. 20:3). If a man loves God, you will not have to tell him that. Love is the fulfilling of that law. " Thou shalt not take the name of Jehovah thy God in vain" (v. 7). Would he ever dream of taking His name in vain if he loved Him? "Remember the sabbath day, to keep it holy" (v. 8). Would he not be too glad to have one day in seven to dedicate more exclusively to the object of his affection? Love would fulfill all these laws regarding God.

And so, if he loved, you would never think of telling him to honor his father and mother. He could not do anything else. It would be preposterous to tell him not to kill. You could only insult him if you suggested that he should not steal. How could he steal from those he loved? It would be superfluous to beg him not to bear false witness against his neighbor. If he loved him it would be the last thing he would do. And you would never dream of urging him not to covet what his neighbors have. He would rather they possessed it than himself. In this way "love is the fulfilling of the law." It is the rule for fulfilling all rules, the new commandment for keeping all the old commandments, and Christ's one *secret of the Christian life.*

Now Paul has learned that. In this noble eulogy he has given us the most wonderful and original account extant of the *summum bonum.* We may divide it into three parts. In the beginning of the short chapter we have love *contrasted.* In the heart of it, we have love *analyzed.* Toward the end, we have love *defended* as the supreme gift.

The Contrast

Paul begins by contrasting love with other things that men in those days thought much of. I shall not attempt to go over these things in detail. Their inferiority is already obvious.

He contrasts it with *eloquence.* And what a noble gift it is, the power of playing upon the souls and wills of men, and rousing them to lofty purposes and holy deeds! Paul says, "If I speak with the tongues of men and of angels, and have not love, I am become sounding brass, or a clanging cymbal" (1 Cor. 13:1). We all know why. We have all felt the brazenness of words without emotion, the hollowness, the unaccountable unpersuasiveness of eloquence behind which lies no love.

He contrasts it with *prophecy*. He contrasts it with *mysteries*. He contrasts it with *faith*. He contrasts it with *charity*. Why is love greater than faith? Because the end is greater than the means. And why is it greater than charity? Because the whole is greater than the part.

Love is greater than *faith,* because the end is greater than the means. What is the use of having faith? It is to connect the soul with God. And what is the object of connecting man with God? That he may become like God. But God is love. Hence faith, the means, is in order to love, the end. Love, therefore, obviously is greater than faith. "If I have all faith, so as to remove mountains, but have not love, I am nothing" (v. 2).

It is greater than *charity,* again, because the whole is greater than a part. Charity is only a little bit of love, one of the innumerable avenues of love. There may even be, and there is, a great deal of charity without love. It is a very easy thing to toss a copper to a beggar on the street. It is generally an easier thing than not to do it. Yet love is just as often in the withholding. We purchase relief from the sympathetic feelings roused by the spectacle of misery at the copper's cost. It is too cheap—too cheap for us—and often too dear for the beggar. If we really loved him, we would either do more for him, or less. Hence, "If I bestow all my goods to feed the poor . . . but have not love, it profiteth me nothing" (v. 3).

Then Paul contrasts it with *sacrifice* and martyrdom: "If I give my body to be burned, but have not love, it profiteth me nothing" (v. 3). Missionaries can take nothing greater to the heathen world than the impress and reflection of the love of God upon their own character. That is the universal language. It will take them years to speak in Chinese or in the dialects of India. From the day they land, that language of love, understood by all, will be pouring forth its unconscious eloquence.

It is the man who is the missionary, not his words. His

character is his message. In the heart of Africa, among the great lakes, I have come across black men and women who remembered the only white man they ever saw before— David Livingstone. As you cross his footsteps in that dark continent, *men's faces light up* as they speak of the kind doctor who passed there years ago. They could not understand him, but they felt the love that beat in his heart. They knew that it was love, although he spoke not a word.

Take into your sphere of labor, where you also mean to lay down your life, that simple charm, and your lifework must succeed. You can take nothing greater, you need take nothing less. You may take every accomplishment and may be braced for every sacrifice, but if you give your body to be burned and have not love, it will profit you and the cause of Christ *nothing*.

The Analysis

After contrasting love with these things, Paul, in three very short verses, gives us an amazing analysis of what this supreme thing is.

I ask you to look at it. It is a compound thing, he tells us. It is like light. As you have seen a man of science take a beam of light and pass it through a crystal prism and have seen it come out on the other side of the prism broken up into its component colors—red and blue and yellow and violet and orange and all the colors of the rainbow—so Paul passes this thing, love, through the magnificent prism of his inspired intellect. Thus, it comes out on the other side broken up into its elements.

In these few words we have what one might call *the spectrum of love,* or the analysis of love. Will you observe what its elements are? Will you notice that they have common names, that they are virtues that we hear about every day, that they are things that can be practiced by every man in every place in life? And will you notice how, by a multitude of small things and ordinary virtues, the supreme thing, the *summum bonum,* is made up?

The spectrum of love that is found in verses 4–6 has nine ingredients:

Patience ...... "Love suffereth long,"
Kindness ..... "and is kind;"
Generosity .... "love envieth not;"
Humility ...... "love vaunteth not itself, is not puffed up,"
Courtesy ...... "doth not behave itself unseemly"
Unselfishness .. "seeketh not its own,"
Good temper ... "is not provoked"
Guilelessness .. "taketh not account of evil;"
Sincerity ...... "rejoiceth not in unrighteousness, but rejoiceth with the truth."

Patience, kindness, generosity, humility, courtesy, unselfishness, good temper, guilelessness, sincerity—these make up the supreme gift, the stature of the perfect man.

You will observe that all are in relation to men, in relation to life, in relation to the known today and the near tomorrow, and not to the unknown eternity. We hear much of love to God; Christ spoke much of love to man. We make a great deal of peace with heaven; Christ made much of peace on earth. Religion is not a strange or added thing, but the inspiration of the secular life, the breathing of an eternal Spirit through this temporal world. The supreme thing, in short, is not a thing at all, but the giving of a further finish to the multitudinous words and acts that make up the sum of every common day.

Patience. This is the normal attitude of love—passive, waiting to begin, not in a hurry, calm. Love is ready to do its work when the summons comes, but in the meantime it wears the ornament of a meek and quiet spirit. "Love suffereth long . . . beareth all things; believeth all things, hopeth all things" (vv. 4, 7). For love understands and therefore waits.

Kindness. Love is active. Have you ever noticed how much of Christ's life was spent in doing kind things—in *merely* doing kind things? Run over it with that in view, and you will find that He spent a great proportion of His time simply in making people happy, in *doing good turns* for people. There is only one thing greater than happiness in the world and that is holiness, and it is not in our keeping. But what God *has* put in our power is the happiness of those about us, and that is largely to be secured by our being kind to them.

"The greatest thing," says someone, "a man can do for his heavenly Father is to be kind to some of His other children." I wonder why it is that we are not all kinder than we are? How much the world needs it! How easily it is done! How instantaneously it acts! How infallibly it is remembered! How superabundantly it pays itself back, for there is no debtor in the world so honorable, so superbly honorable, as love. "Love never faileth" (v. 8). Love is success, love is happiness, love is life. "Love," I say with Browning, "is energy of life."

> For life, with all it yields of joy or woe
>   And hope and fear,
> Is just our chance o' the prize of learning love,—
> How love might be, hath been indeed, and is.

Where love is, God is. "He that dwelleth in love dwelleth in God" (1 John 4:16 KJV). God is love, therefore, *love*. Without distinction, without calculation, without procrastination, love. Lavish it upon the poor, where it is very easy. Lavish it especially upon the rich, who often need it most. Most of all, lavish it upon our equals, where it is very difficult and for whom perhaps we each do least of all. There is a difference between *trying to please* and *giving pleasure*. Give pleasure. Lose no chance of giving pleasure, for that is the ceaseless and anonymous triumph of a truly loving spirit. "I shall pass through this world but once. Any good thing, therefore, that I can do, or any kindness that I can show to any human being, let me do it now. Let me not defer it or neglect it, for I shall not pass this way again."

Generosity. "Love envieth not." This is love in competition with others. Whenever you attempt a good work you will find other men doing the same kind of work, and probably doing it better. Envy them not. Envy is a feeling of ill-will to those who are in the same line as ourselves, a spirit of covetousness and detraction. How little Christian work even is a protection against un-Christian feeling! That most despicable of all the unworthy moods that cloud a Christian's soul assuredly waits for us on the threshold of every work, unless we are fortified with this grace of magnanimity. Only one thing truly need the Christian envy—the large, rich, generous soul that "envieth not."

And then, after having learned all that, you have to learn this further thing: *humility*—to put a seal upon your lips and forget what you have done. After you have been kind, after love has stolen forth into the world and done its beautiful work, go back into the shade again and say nothing about it. Love hides even from itself. Love waives even self-satisfaction. "Love vaunteth not itself, is not puffed up." Humility is love hiding.

The fifth ingredient, *courtesy,* is a somewhat strange one to find in this *summum bonum*. This is love in society, in relation to etiquette. "Love . . . doth not behave itself unseemly."

Politeness has been defined as "love in trifles." Courtesy is said to be love in little things. And the one secret of politeness is to love.

Love *cannot* behave itself unseemly. You can put the most untutored persons into the highest society, and if they have a reservoir of love in their heart they will not behave unseemly. They simply cannot do it. Carlyle said of Robert Burns that there was no truer gentleman in Europe than the plowman-poet. It was because he loved everything—the mouse and the daisy and all the things, great and small, that God had made. So with this simple passport he could mingle with any society, and enter courts and palaces from his little cottage on the banks of the Ayr.

You know the meaning of the word "gentleman." It means a gentle man—a man who does things gently with love. That is the whole art and mystery of it. The gentle man cannot in the nature of things do an ungentle, an ungentlemanly thing. The ungentle soul, the inconsiderate, unsympathetic nature, cannot do anything else. "Love . . . doth not behave itself unseemly."

Unselfishness. Love "seeketh not its own." Observe: Seeks not even that which is her own. In Britain the

Englishman is devoted, and rightly, to his rights. But there come times when a man may exercise even *the higher right* of giving up his rights.

Yet Paul does not summon us to give up our rights. Love strikes much deeper. It would have us not seek them at all, but rather ignore them. It would have us eliminate the personal element altogether from our calculations.

It is not hard to give up our rights. They are often eternal. The difficult thing is to give up *ourselves*. The more difficult thing still is not to seek things for ourselves at all. After we have sought them, bought them, won them, deserved them, we have taken the cream off them for ourselves already. Little cross then to give them up. But not to seek them, to look every man not on his own things, but on the things of others—that is the difficulty. "Seekest thou great things for thyself? seek them not," said the prophet (Jer. 45:5). Why? Because there is no greatness in things. Things cannot be great. The only greatness is unselfish love. Even self-denial in itself is nothing and is almost a mistake. Only a great purpose or a mightier love can justify the waste.

It is more difficult, I have said, not to seek our own at all than, having sought it, to give it up. I must take that back. It is only true of a partly selfish heart. Nothing is a hardship to love, and nothing is hard. I believe that Christ's "yoke" is easy. Christ's yoke is just His way of taking life. And I believe it is an easier way than any other. I believe it is a happier way than any other. The most obvious lesson in Christ's teaching is that there is no happiness in having and getting anything, but only in giving. I repeat, there is no happiness in having or in getting, but only in giving. Half the world is on the wrong scent in pursuit of happiness. They think it consists in having and getting, and in being served by others. It consists in giving and in serving others. "He that would be great among you," said Christ, "let him serve." He who would be happy, let him remember that there is but one way: "It is more blessed [it is more happy] to give than to receive" (Acts 20:35).

The next ingredient is a very remarkable one: *good temper*. "Love . . . is not provoked." Nothing could be more striking than to find this here. We are inclined to look upon a bad temper as a very harmless weakness. We speak of it as a mere infirmity of nature, a family failing, a matter of temperament, not a thing to take into very serious account in estimating a man's character. And yet here, right in the heart of this analysis of love, it finds a place. The Bible again and again returns to condemn it as one of the most destructive elements in human nature.

The peculiarity of an ill temper is that it is the vice of the virtuous. It is often the one blot on an otherwise noble character. You know men who are all but perfect, and women who would be entirely perfect, but for an easily ruffled, quick-tempered, or "touchy" disposition. This compatibility of an ill temper with high moral character is one of the strangest and saddest problems of ethics. The truth is, there are two great classes of sins: sins of the *body* and sins of the *disposition*. The prodigal son may be taken as a type of the first, the elder brother of the second.

Now, society has no doubt whatever as to which of these is the worse. Its brand falls, without a challenge, upon the prodigal. But are we right? We have no balance to weigh one another's sins, and coarser and finer are but human words. But faults in the higher nature may be less venal than those in the lower, and to the eye of Him who is love, a sin against love may seem a hundred times more base. No form of vice—not worldliness, not greed of gold, not drunkenness itself—does more to un-Christianize society than evil temper. For embittering life, for breaking up communities, for destroying the most sacred relationships, for devastating homes, for withering up men and women, for taking the bloom of childhood, in short, *for sheer gratuitous misery-producing power,* this influence stands alone.

Look at the elder brother—moral, hard-working, patient, dutiful—let him get all credit for his virtues. But look at this man, this baby, sulking outside his own father's door. "He was angry," we read, "and would not go in" (Luke 15:28a). Look at the effect upon the father, upon the servants, upon the happiness of the guests. Judge of the effect upon the prodigal—and how many prodigals are kept out of the kingdom of God by the unlovely character of those who profess to be inside. Analyze, as a study in temper, the thundercloud itself as it gathers upon the elder brother's brow. What is it made of? Jealousy, anger, pride, uncharity, cruelty, self-righteousness, touchiness, doggedness, sullenness—these are the ingredients of this dark and loveless soul. In varying proportions, also, these are the ingredients of all ill temper.

Judge if such sins of the disposition are not worse to live in, and for others to live with, than the sins of the body. Did Christ indeed not answer the question Himself when He said, "I say unto you, that the publicans and the harlots go into the kingdom of God before you" (Matt. 21:31b)? There is really no place in heaven for a disposition like this. A man with such a mood could only make heaven miserable for all the people in it. Except, therefore, such a man be *born again,* he cannot, simply *cannot,* enter the kingdom of heaven.

You will see then why temper is significant. It is not in what it is alone, but in what it reveals. This is why I speak of it with such unusual plainness. It is a test for love, a symptom, a revelation of an unloving nature at bottom. It is the intermittent fever that bespeaks unintermittent disease within. It is the occasional bubble escaping to the surface that betrays some rottenness underneath. It is a sample of the most hidden products of the soul dropped involuntarily when off one's guard. In a word, the lightning form of a hundred hideous and unchristian sins. A want of patience, a want of kindness, a want of generosity, a want of courtesy, a want of unselfishness are all instantaneously symbolized in one flash of temper.

Hence it is not enough to deal with the temper. We must go to the source and change the inmost nature, and the angry humors will die away of themselves. Souls are made sweet not by taking the acid fluids out, but by putting something in—a great love, a new Spirit, the Spirit of Christ. Christ, the Spirit of Christ, interpenetrating ours sweetens, purifies, transforms all. This only can eradicate what is wrong, work a chemical change, renovate and regenerate, and rehabilitate the inner man. Willpower does not change men. Time does not change men. *Christ does.* Therefore, "Let this mind be in you, which was also in Christ Jesus" (Phil. 2:5 KJV).

Some of us have not much time to lose. Remember, once more, that this is a matter of life or death. I cannot help speaking urgently, for myself or for yourselves. "Whoso shall offend one of these little ones which believe in me, it were better for him that a millstone were hanged about his neck, and that he were drowned in the depth of the sea" (Matt. 18:6 KJV). That is to say, it is the deliberate verdict of the Lord Jesus that it is better not to live than not to love. *It is better not to live than not to love.*

Guilelessness and *sincerity* may be dismissed almost without a word. Guilelessness is the grace for suspicious people. The possession of it is *the great secret of personal influence.*

You will find, if you think for a moment, that the people who influence you are people who believe in you. In an atmosphere of suspicion men shrivel up, but in that atmosphere they expand, and find encouragement and educative fellowship.

It is a wonderful thing that here and there in this hard, uncharitable world there should still be left a few rare souls who think no evil. This is the great unworldliness. Love "thinketh no evil" (KJV), imputes no motive, sees the bright side, puts the best construction on every action. What a delightful state of mind to live in! What a stimulus and benediction even to meet with it for a day! To be trusted is to be saved. And if we try to influence or elevate others, we shall soon see that success is in proportion to their belief of our belief in them. The respect of another is the first restoration of the self-respect a man has lost. Our ideal of what he is becomes to him the hope and pattern of what he may become.

Love "rejoiceth not in unrighteousness, but rejoiceth with the truth." I have called this *sincerity* from the words rendered in the Authorized Version by "rejoiceth in the truth." And, certainly, were this the real translation, nothing could be more just, for he who loves will love truth not less than men. He will rejoice in the truth—rejoice not in what he has been taught to believe, not in this church's doctrine or in that, not in this "ism" or in that "ism," but "in *the truth*." He will accept only what is real. He will strive to get at facts. He will search for *truth* with a humble and unbiased mind, and cherish whatever he finds at any sacrifice.

But the more literal translation of the Revised Version calls for just such a sacrifice for truth's sake here. For what Paul really meant is, as we there read, "Rejoiceth not in unrighteousness, but rejoiceth with the truth," a quality which probably no one English word—and certainly not *sincerity*—adequately defines. It includes, perhaps more strictly, the self-restraint that refuses to make capital out of others' faults; the charity that delights not in exposing the weakness of others, but "covereth all things" (v. 7 RV); the sincerity of purpose that endeavors to see things as they are, and rejoices to find them better than suspicion feared or calumny denounced.

So much for the analysis of love. Now the business of our lives is to have these things fitted into our characters. That is the supreme work to which we need to address ourselves in this world—to learn love. Is life not full of opportunities for learning love? Every man and woman every day has a thousand of them. The world is not a playground, it is a schoolroom. Life is not a holiday, but an education. And *the one eternal lesson* for us all is *how better we can love*.

What makes a man a good cricketer? Practice. What makes a man a good artist, a good sculptor, a good musician? Practice. What makes a man a good linguist, a good stenographer? Practice. What makes a man a good man? Practice. Nothing else. There is nothing capricious about religion. We do not get the soul in different ways, under different laws, from those in which we get the body and the mind. If a man does not exercise his arm, he develops no biceps muscle. If a man does not exercise his soul, he acquires no muscle in his soul, no strength of character, no vigor of moral fiber, no beauty of spiritual growth. Love is not a thing of enthusiastic emotion. It is a rich, strong, manly, vigorous expression of the whole round Christian character—the Christlike nature in its fullest development. And the constituents of this great character are only to be built up by *ceaseless practice.*

What was Christ doing in the carpenter's shop? Practicing. Though perfect, we read that He *learned* obedience, and grew in wisdom and in favor with God. Do not quarrel, therefore, with your lot in life. Do not complain of its never-ceasing cares, its petty environment, the vexations you have to stand, the small and sordid souls you have to live and work with. Above all, do not resent temptation. Do not be perplexed because it seems to thicken around you more and more, and ceases neither for effort nor for agony nor for prayer. That is your practice. That is the practice which God appoints you, and it is having its work in making you patient, humble, generous, unselfish, kind, and courteous. Do not grudge the hand that is molding the still too shapeless image within you. It is growing more beautiful, though you see it not. Every touch of temptation may add to its perfection, therefore, keep in the midst of life. Do not isolate yourself. Be among men and among things, and among troubles and difficulties and obstacles. You remember Goethe's words: "Talent develops itself in solitude; character in the stream of life." Talent develops itself in solitude—the talent of prayer, of faith, of meditation, of seeing the unseen; character grows in the stream of the world's life. That chiefly is where men are to learn love.

How? Now, how? To make it easier, I have named a few of the elements of love. But these are only elements. Love itself can never be defined. Light is something more than the sum of its ingredients—a glowing, dazzling, tremulous ether. And love is something more than all its elements—a palpitating, quivering, sensitive, living thing. By synthesis of all the colors, men can make whiteness; they cannot make light. By synthesis of all the virtues, men can make virtue; they cannot make love. How then are we to have this transcendent, living whole conveyed into our souls? We brace our wills to secure it. We try to copy those who have it. We lay down rules about it. We watch. We pray. But these things alone will not bring love into our nature. Love is an *effect*. And only as we fulfill the right condition can we have the effect produced. Shall I tell you what the *cause* is?

If you turn to the Revised Version of 1 John you find these words: "We love because He first loved us." "We love," not "We love *Him*." That is the way the old version has it, and it is quite wrong. "*We love*—because He first loved us." Look at that word "because." It is the *cause* of which I have spoken. "*Because* He first loved us," the effect follows that we love, we love Him, we love all men. We cannot help it. Because He loved us, we love, we love everybody. Our heart is slowly changed. Contemplate the love of Christ, and you will love. Stand before that mirror, reflect Christ's character, and you will be changed into the same image from tenderness to tenderness. There is no other way. You cannot love to order. You can only look at the lovely object, fall in love with it, and grow into likeness to it. And so look at this Perfect Character, this Perfect Life. Look at *the great sacrifice* as He laid down Himself, all through life, and upon the cross of Calvary. You must love Him. And loving Him, you most become like Him.

Love begets love. It is a process of induction. Put a piece of iron in the presence of an electrified body, and that piece of iron for a time becomes electrified. It is changed into a temporary magnet in the mere presence of a permanent magnet, and as long as you leave the two side by side, they are both magnets alike. Remain side by side with Him who loved us, and *gave Himself for us,* and you, too, will become a permanent magnet, a permanently attractive force. Like Him you will draw all men to you, and like Him you will be drawn to all men. That is the inevitable effect of love. Any man who fulfills that cause must have that effect produced in him.

Try to give up the idea that religion comes to us by chance, or by mystery, or by caprice. It comes to us by natural law or by supernatural law, for all law is divine.

Edward Irving went to see a dying boy once, and when he entered the room he just put his hand on the sufferer's head and said, "My boy, God loves you," and went away. The boy started from his bed and called out to the people in the house, "God loves me! God loves me!"

One word! It changed that boy. The sense that God loved him overpowered him, melted him down, and began the creating of a new heart in him. And that is how the love of God melts down the unlovely heart in man and begets in him the new creature, who is patient and humble and gentle and unselfish. And there is no other way to get it. There is no mystery about it. We love others, we love everybody, we love our enemies, *because He first loved us.*

The Defense

Now I have a closing sentence or two to add about Paul's reason for singling out love as the supreme possession. It is a very remarkable reason. In a single word it is this: *It lasts.* "Love," urges Paul, "never faileth" (v. 8). Then he begins again one of his marvelous lists of the great things of the day, and exposes them one by one. He runs over the things that men thought were going to last, and shows that they are all fleeting, temporary, passing away.

"Whether there be *prophecies,* they shall be done away" (v. 8). It was the mother's ambition for her boy in those days that he should become a prophet. For hundreds of years God had never spoken by means of any prophet, and at that time the prophet was greater than the king. Men waited wistfully for another messenger to come and hung upon his lips when he appeared, as upon the very voice of God. Paul says, "Whether there be prophecies, they shall [fail]." The Bible is full of prophecies. One by one they have "failed," that is, having been fulfilled, their work is finished. They have nothing more to do now in the world except to feed a devout man's faith.

Then Paul talks about *tongues*. That was another thing that was greatly coveted. "Whether there be tongues, they shall cease" (v. 8). As we all know, many, many centuries have passed since tongues have been known in this world. They have ceased. Take it in any sense you like. Take it, for illustration merely, as languages in general—a sense which was not in Paul's mind at all, and which, though it cannot give us the specific lesson, will point the general truth. Consider the words in which these chapters were written—Greek. It has gone. Take the Latin—the other great tongue of those days. It ceased long ago. Look at the Indian language. It is ceasing. The language of Wales, of Ireland, of the Scottish Highlands is dying before our eyes. The most popular book in the English tongue at the present time, except the Bible, is one of Dickens' works, his *Pickwick Papers*. It is largely written in the language of London street life. And experts assure us that in fifty years it will be unintelligible to the average English reader.

Then Paul goes further, and with even greater boldness adds, "Whether there be knowledge, it shall be done away" (v. 8). The wisdom of the ancients, where is it? It is wholly gone. A schoolboy today knows more than Sir Isaac Newton knew. His knowledge has vanished away. You put yesterday's newspaper in the fire, and its knowledge has vanished away. You buy the old editions of the great encyclopedias for a few cents. Their knowledge has vanished away. Look how the coach has been superseded by the use of steam. Look how electricity has superseded that, and swept a hundred almost new inventions into oblivion. One of the greatest living authorities, Sir William Thompson, said in Scotland at a meeting at which I was present, "The steam engine is passing away." "Whether there be knowledge, it shall [vanish away]." At every workshop you will see in the backyard a heap of old iron, a few wheels, a few levers, a few cranks, broken and eaten with rust. Twenty years ago that was the pride of the city. Men flocked in from the country to see the great invention. Now it is superseded, its day is done. And all the boasted science and philosophy of this day will soon be old.

In my time, in the University of Edinburgh, the greatest figure in the faculty was Sir James Simpson, the discoverer of chloroform. Recently his successor and nephew, Professor Simpson, was asked by the librarian of the university to go to the library and pick out the books on his subject (midwifery) that were no longer needed. His reply to the librarian was this: "Take every textbook that is more than ten years old and put it down in the cellar."

Sir James Simpson was a great authority only a few years ago. Men came from all parts of the earth to consult him, and almost the whole teaching of that time is consigned by the science of today to oblivion. And in every branch of science it is the same. "For we know in part. ... We see through a glass, darkly" (vv. 9, 12 KJV). Knowledge does not last.

Can you tell me anything that is going to last? Many things Paul did not condescend to name. He did not mention money, fortune, or fame. But he picked out the great things of his time, the things the best men thought had something in them, and brushed them peremptorily aside. Paul had no charge against these things in themselves. All he said about them was that they would not last. They were great things, but not supreme things. There were things beyond them. What we are stretches past what we do, beyond what we possess. Many things that men denounce as sins are not sins, but they are temporary. And that is a favorite argument of the New Testament. John says of the world, not that it is wrong, but simply that it "passeth away" (1 John 2:17). There is a great deal in the world that is delightful and beautiful. There is a great deal in it that is great and engrossing, but *it will not last*. All that is in the world, the lust of the eye, the lust of the flesh, and the pride of life, are but for a little while. Love not the world therefore. Nothing that it contains is worth the life and consecration of an immortal soul. The immortal soul must give itself to something that is immortal. And the only immortal things are these: "Now abideth faith, hope, love, these three; and the greatest of these is love."

Some think the time may come when two of these three things will also pass away—faith into sight, hope into fruition. Paul does not say so. We know but little now about the conditions of the life that is to come. But what is certain is that love must last. God, the Eternal God, is love. Covet, therefore, that everlasting gift, that one thing which it is certain is going to stand, that one coinage that will be current in the universe when all the other coinages of all the nations of the world shall be useless and unhonored. You will give yourselves to many things, give yourself first to love. Hold things in their proportion. *Hold things in their proportion.* Let at least the first great object of our lives be to achieve the character defended in these words, the character—and it is the character of Christ—that is built around love.

I have said this thing is eternal. Did you ever notice how continually John associates love and faith with eternal life? I was not told when I was a boy that "God so loved the world, that he gave his only begotten Son, that whosoever believeth on him should . . . have eternal life" (John 3:16). What I was told, I remember, was that God so loved the world that, if I trusted in Him, I was to have a thing called peace, or I was to have rest, or I was to have joy, or I was to have safety. But I had to find out for myself that whosoever trusts in Him—that is, whosoever loves Him, for trust is only the avenue to love—has everlasting life.

The Gospel offers a man a life. Never offer a man a thimbleful of Gospel. Do not offer them merely joy, or merely peace, or merely rest, or merely safety. Tell them how Christ came to give men a more abundant life than they have. Tell them how it is a life abundant in love and, therefore, abundant in salvation for themselves, and large in enterprise for the alleviation and redemption of the world. Then only can the Gospel take hold of the whole of a man—body, soul, and spirit—and give to each part of his nature its exercise and reward. Many of the current gospels are addressed only to a part of man's nature. They offer peace, not life; faith, not love; justification, not regeneration. And men slip back again from such religion because the popular gospel has never really held them. Their nature was not all in it. It offered no deeper and gladder life-current than the life that was lived before. Surely it stands to reason that only a fuller love can compete with the love of the world.

To love abundantly is to live abundantly, and to love forever is to live forever. Hence, eternal life is inextricably bound up with love. We want to live forever for the same reason that we want to live tomorrow. Why do we want to live tomorrow? Is it because there is someone who loves you, whom you want to see tomorrow and be with and love back? There is no other reason why we should live on than that we love and are beloved. It is when a man has no one to love him that he commits suicide. So long as he has friends, those who love him and whom he loves, he will live because to live is to love. Be it but the love of a dog, it will keep him in life. But let that go, he has no contact with life, no reason to live. He dies by his own hand.

Eternal life also is to know God, and God is love. This is Christ's own definition. Ponder it. "This is life eternal, that they might know thee the only true God, and Jesus Christ, whom thou hast sent" (John 17:3 KJV). Love must be eternal. It is what God is. On the last analysis, then, love is life. Love never fails, and life never fails, so long as there is love. That is the philosophy of what Paul is showing us. The reason why in the nature of things love should be the supreme thing is because it is going to last and because in the nature of things it is an eternal life. It is a thing that we are living now, not that we get when we die, and that we shall have a poor chance of getting when we die unless we are living now.

No worse fate can befall a man in this world than to live and grow old alone, unloving and unloved. To be lost is to live in an unregenerate condition, loveless and unloved. To be saved is to love. He that dwells in love dwells already in God. For God is love.

Now I have all but finished. How many of you will join me in reading this chapter once a week for the next three months? A man did that once and it changed his whole life. Will you do it? It is for the greatest thing in the world. You might begin by reading it every day, especially the verses that describe the perfect character. "Love suffereth long, and is kind; love envieth not; love vaunteth not itself." Get these ingredients into your life. Then everything that you do is eternal. It is worth doing. It is worth giving time to. No man can become a saint in his sleep. To fulfill the condition required demands a certain amount of prayer and meditation and time, just as improvement in any direction, bodily or mental, requires preparation and care. Address yourselves to that one thing. At any cost have this transcendent character exchanged for yours.

You will find as you look back upon your life that the moments that stand out, the moments when you have really lived, are the moments when you have done things in a spirit of love. As memory scans the past, above and beyond all the transitory pleasures of life, there leap forward those supreme hours when you have been enabled to do unnoticed kindnesses to those around you—things too trifling to speak about, but which you feel have entered into your eternal life. I have seen almost all the beautiful things God has made and have enjoyed almost every pleasure that He has planned for man, yet as I look back I see, standing out above all the life that has gone, four or five short experiences when the love of God reflected itself in some poor imitation, some small act of love of mine, and these seem to be the things which alone of all one's life abide. Everything else in all our lives is transitory. Every other good is vision. But the acts of love that no man knows about, or can ever know about, they never fail.

In the book of Matthew, where the judgment day is depicted for us in the imagery of One seated upon a throne and dividing the sheep from the goats, the test of a man then is not, "How have I believed?" but "How have I loved?" The test of religion, the final test of religion, is not religiousness, but love. I say the final test of religion at that great day is not religiousness, but love. It is not what I have done, not what I have believed, not what I have achieved, but how I have discharged the common charities of life. Sins of commission in that awful indictment are not even referred to. By what we have not done, *by sins of omission,* we are judged. It could not be otherwise. For the withholding of love is the negation of the Spirit of Christ. It is the proof that we never knew Him and that for us He lived in vain. It means that He suggested nothing in all our thoughts, that He inspired nothing in all our lives, that we were not once near enough to Him to be seized with the spell of His compassion for the world. It means that—

> I lived for myself, I thought for myself,
> For myself, and none beside—
> Just as if Jesus had never lived,
> As if He had never died.

Thank God the Christianity of today is coming nearer the world's need. Live to help that on. Thank God men know better, by a hair's breadth, what religion is, what God is, who Christ is, where Christ is. Who is Christ? He who fed the hungry, clothed the naked, visited the sick. And where is Christ? Where? "Whoso shall receive one such little child in my name receiveth me" (Matt. 18:5). And who are Christ's? "Every one that loveth is born of God" (1 John 4:7 KJV).

NOTES